Readers' Advisory for Children and 'Tweens

Readers' Advisory for Children and 'Tweens

Penny Peck

LIBRARIES UNLIMITED

AN IMPRINT OF ABC-CLIO, LLC
Santa Barbara, California • Denver, Colorado • Oxford, England

Library of Congress Cataloging-in-Publication Data

Peck, Penny.
  Readers' advisory for children and 'tweens / Penny Peck.
    p. cm.
  Includes bibliographical references and index.
  ISBN 978-1-59884-387-3 (pbk. : acid-free paper) — ISBN
  978-1-59884-388-0 (ebook) 1. Readers' advisory services—United
  States. 2. Children—Books and reading—United States. 3.
  Preteens—Books and reading—United States. 4. Children's
  libraries—United States—Book lists. 5. School libraries—United
  States—Book lists. I. Title.
  Z711.55P43 2010
  025.5'4—dc22   2010002589

ISBN: 978-1-59884-387-3
E-ISBN: 978-1-59884-388-0

14 13 12 11 10 1 2 3 4 5

This book is also available on the World Wide Web as an eBook.
Visit www.abc-clio.com for details.

Libraries Unlimited
An Imprint of ABC-Clio, LLC

ABC-CLIO, LLC
130 Cremona Drive, P.O. Box 1911
Santa Barbara, California 93116-1911

This book is printed on acid-free paper ∞
Manufactured in the United States of America

Special thanks to the Association of
Children's Librarians of Northern California

Contents

Introduction

When I went to graduate school for my master's in library science degree, readers' advisory was considered an essential skill for children's librarians. Of course, that was before the advent of personal computers! Now library employees have many other responsibilities, from running computer labs, to maintaining homework centers, to managing branch libraries with just one or two employees. So readers' advisory for children and 'tweens sometimes gets lost in the shuffle, and it can be unfamiliar to many library staff members. Many of us still think of it as a key skill of youth services library staff, but in many cases it is learned on the job. This book aims to help in that goal, to assist you with youth readers' advisory skills so that readers' advisory can become one of the main talents you bring to the job.

Maybe you are a longtime adult reference librarian, who now has to work at the children's desk as a result of cutbacks. Or you are a new staff member at an elementary school library that can no longer afford a credentialed librarian. Or you are the young adult librarian who was recently promoted to head of youth services and are quickly learning how to assist younger children. Or you are a new librarian, interested in youth services and children's books, but haven't had much experience yet. All of these scenarios are examples of situations in which you can benefit from this book.

When I started as a children's librarian twenty-five years ago, we still worked with the card catalog. And I was expected to read a good portion of the collection so I could recommend books to children. Now many children's librarians have to manage several employees, write grants, and perform other duties that minimize the amount of time they have to read. Luckily there are Web sites and books that can help with readers' advisory; many are recommended in the following chapters. Even if you haven't read a particular book, you can still recommend it to a young person—you just need to know something about that book. Of course reading as many of the books in your collection as possible is still important and will help you better serve young readers, but sometimes reading every title is impossible. That's where other skills and tools come in.

Some of you may wonder about the use of the word *'tween* in the title of this book. As of this writing, 'tween is starting to become the accepted term when referring to young people between the ages of nine and twelve—they are truly preteen, but not a small child who needs babysitting. 'Tweens are upper elementary and middle school students who have some independence; they often visit the library on the way home from school, without a parent or caregiver. They are a huge market, spending considerable amounts of money on popular culture items, from "Spongebob" backpacks to Jonas Brothers music CDs. This book provides details on assisting them in finding recreational reading, so they will continue to enjoy reading and not just read for homework.

Serving younger children is also addressed in this book, from assisting parents and preschoolers who want to find picture books, to helping kindergarteners and first graders find easy readers they can tackle on their own, to encouraging second and third graders to move up from easy readers to transitional fiction, which are shorter chapter books, to the full-fledged novels they will read as 'tweens. There are chapters focusing on each of these types of books, going into more detail on how to help children find books that are a good "fit" for them and packed with lists of additional books.

Your library may not own every book mentioned in this guide. But it is likely to carry some of these books, which are often very popular and may have been requested anyway. If your library needs to add books to meet readers' advisory demands, consider purchasing paperback copies of some of the more popular books mentioned here so you have something on hand when it is time to do readers' advisory. This book also lists helpful Web sites that offer even more titles you can recommend, especially for the "fussy" reader who doesn't seem tempted by any of your recommendations.

Readers' advisory can and should include nonfiction, folklore, poetry, and graphic novels as well fiction. Many young people enjoy these types of books for recreational reading. You'll also find some tips on promoting books, from booktalking, to booklists, to displays, to programming ideas. There should be something here even for longtime children's librarians looking to freshen up their readers' advisory repertoire. You may even find books here that you want to read yourself!

As you begin to explore this book, you may want to start a file or database of these titles, so you have them at your fingertips when it is time to do some readers' advisory. How you use the book is up to you; it was written to assist the many people dedicated to helping children in the library and to make that job easier. With so many libraries facing cutbacks, many of us need to learn new skills and serve a wider variety of patrons, including young people, and this book is intended to help face that challenge.

Chapter 1

Readers' Advisory

If you work at a library, you may have been the type of child who read after bedtime, with a flashlight under the covers. Reading and talking about books is one reason many of us joined the library profession, whether as a librarian or one of the vital support staff who works at the children's desk. Helping a person find the answer to a homework question is often straightforward, but finding books a child or 'tween might like is a more nuanced and subjective skill.

This first chapter covers some basic skills needed to diagnose what a young reader might like. If you were a waiter, you wouldn't automatically order a dish for a customer without first asking about that person's likes and dislikes, allergies, or other needs. It's the same with readers' advisory: you want to find out a little about the person before offering recreational reading suggestions.

Connecting children with books that will soon become their favorites can be very rewarding. Library staff and volunteers at all levels, from the library aides who shelve books to the library director, probably came to work in a library because they loved reading. So doing readers' advisory may tap into your passion for books. You don't have to have read every book in the children's room to do readers' advisory, but it does require some knowledge of books and children, as well as interpersonal communication skills, like being a good listener and being patient.

1

Definition of Readers' Advisory

Readers' advisory is usually thought of as finding recreational reading, as opposed to finding books for homework assignments or books on how to draw or play a sport, for example. So readers' advisory often means finding fiction books for the customer, similar to hand-selling in an independent bookstore. It can be very challenging, like picking out clothes for someone you don't know. This can be made even more difficult if the child the books are for is not there. Sometimes parents are at the library to pick up books for their children, but the children aren't there to add their input. This makes readers' advisory more difficult, but not impossible.

Children are often more flexible in their recreational reading than adults. We all have an aunt or grandmother who only reads mysteries, but a child who is a huge fantasy or <u>Harry Potter</u> fan may be willing to try historical novels such as Laura Ingalls Wilder's <u>Little House</u> series or an animal story such as Wilson Rawls's *Where the Red Fern Grows*. Because children are curious, they often take chances with their reading choices.

Understanding Readers

When children are your customers, it can be helpful to understand some basics of child development to serve them better. There can be some developmental reasons for children's inability to express their needs or to work efficiently in the library. Knowing a few facts about child development can help us be better listeners and more patient with younger customers. It can also remove the filter between you and the child and make your interactions more effective.

It is often determined by child development specialists that children under the age of eight cannot always tell right from wrong or tell reality from imagination. That is why age eight is referred to as "the age of reason" for children to be able to be on their own. Many libraries will have a policy that children must be at least eight to be in the library without adult supervision. These rules are based on child development principles. Those who work with children will notice that they may have to tell a five-year-old the same rules over and over, but a nine-year-old may remember from one minute to the next that there is a rule against running in the library. If the five-year-olds forget, you have to remind them every time they come to the library. Therefore, when the child is younger than eight, the readers' advisor often talks to both the parent and child.

Early childhood is ages three to eight, an age group that is usually in the library with a parent or caregiver. This age group takes great pride in accomplishments, so let them help in finding books they request; even if they cannot type, let them watch you use the online catalog. Partner with them to help them find what they are requesting instead of just handing it to them.

Later childhood is ages nine to twelve. Children in this category will often go to the library without an adult; this is the group referred to as 'tweens. If an adult does come to the library with a 'tween, often the child will separate from the adult when it comes time to ask for materials. Children in this age group are very good at concrete problem solving, are industrious, and take initiative. These children like to use online computers to find their own materials or may want you to just assist while they take the lead. Partner with 'tweens when doing readers' advisory, and they are more likely to accept your suggestions.

Adolescents, or teens, enjoy making their own decisions. Parents and other adults, including librarians and teachers, can show them the results of their search and help them choose again for different results if that is what is needed, but teens are trying to separate from childhood and show their independence. They often need time to daydream, and may be forgetful, but they will appreciate any adult help that comes across as nonjudgmental. 'Tweens often have many of these characteristics, too.

Brain Development

Recent studies on brain development in babies and very young children have been featured prominently in news magazines and on television. A great deal of pressure is placed on parents to, from day one, read to babies and help them develop language skills, use their imaginations, be stimulated visually and with music, and challenge themselves. Parents may ask for books on physics for a three-year-old. The library can help by offering great picture books, music CDs for children, and CD-ROM learning games that are age appropriate, as well as parenting books. But preschoolers still do not have the fine motor skills needed to keyboard, and parents may need to be helped to learn what their children, even the most advanced, can and cannot be expected to do. Then these parents should be prepared to help their children with tasks they are capable of doing rather than frustrating them with tasks they cannot do. Also, every child in a particular age group is not at the same developmental level, so a great rule of thumb is to be flexible and let parents determine what books would be the best "fit" for their children.

Children and Their Needs

Studies by Abraham Maslow, Erik Erikson, or Jean Piaget provide more information about child development in general. Basically, each of these authors outlined a hierarchy of needs in childhood. A summary of what may fit a child, depending on his or her age, is that children under age six are trying to achieve autonomy, children ages six to nine are developing initiative, those ages nine to twelve are becoming industrious, and teens are establishing their identity. That is one reason preschoolers frequently say "No!"; they are establishing autonomy. Teens may seem rude, but don't take it personally; they are defining who they are.

Children and Choices

Just like adults, children should be offered choices while in the library. Let them look at books both above and below their grade level and see what they choose. Children will often choose nonfiction books that may be too difficult to read from cover to cover, but will serve a need because the photographs are well done. If you provide choices, children are more likely to leave with something; if you only offer one book, there is a greater chance that it won't be what they want, and they will leave empty handed.

Reader Response Theory

There is a new push by teachers to allow children to choose what they want to read, rather than assigning everyone the same book to read. Librarians have done this for a long time, but educators have done research to show that this allows for more growth by the reader. Nancie Atwell's *The Reading Zone* outlines this theory, which is often referred to as "reader response theory." According to this theory, readers respond better to books when they are allowed to choose what to read; reading ability also increases. Readers bring meaning to the texts; a reader's background influences what the text means to that person. So allowing the reader to choose what to read is essential. That is one reason the readers' advisory experience is a partnership between you and the reader; you work together to find books that person may enjoy. Asking children and 'tweens to name books they have already read and enjoyed is one way to use reader response theory to ascertain what books they might enjoy in the future. By celebrating their enthusiasm for books they mention, you can make young readers feel validated. They will listen to your suggestions if you respond positively to the books they say they like.

Preparing to Do Readers' Advisory

If you are expected to do readers' advisory with youth, there are many things you can do to keep up on new titles, familiarize yourself with popular materials, and discover what offerings will be successful. You have already started by reading this manual. Many library staff also regularly read professional journals such as *Horn Book, School Library Journal, Kirkus, Booklist,* and *Publishers Weekly* to follow the trends in books for youth.

Looking over the new books for children and 'tweens before they are put out on the shelves is a great shortcut to keeping up with what your library has. Look at the new children's books regularly and make a note of authors you see often or types of novels you see in abundance, such as fantasy or popular nonfiction topics. You may not have time to read all the new books, but you can look at the book jackets and read the inside flaps to find out what they are about so you can offer them when doing readers' advisory.

Another way to discover what is popular and in demand is to observe what books for children and 'tweens are regularly being reserved and what appears regularly on the return shelves. This can be a quick and easy way to see what is popular in your community.

Familiarize yourself with the children's paperback books; 'tweens often prefer them for recreational reading. See which series you own and which paperbacks look worn; these are often the most popular.

Finally, shelf-read areas in the children's section to see which books are popular. If a shelf looks in pristine condition, it may not contain books in demand (unless a page just did shelf-reading in that section). Notice shelves in disarray; these often contain books in demand. Shelves that are messy is one indicator that the library is being used, and that the particular area contains popular materials. Straighten and shelf-read that area so it is presentable for the next customer, but keep it in mind the next time you do readers' advisory.

Readers' Advisory Interview

When being asked for reading recommendations, first find out if the book will be read for fun or used for homework. If it is for homework, the teacher may have said the book had to be at least a certain length, perhaps 100 pages, or about a certain topic. The teacher also may have specified it be from a list, or that it be a Newbery-winning novel. A teacher may also specify that it be a mystery, or historical fiction, or a "classic";

determining if the request is for a book report for school leads you to regular reference interview questions, such as "Do you have the handout from your teacher describing the assignment?" Sometimes, even when reading for "fun," children need a book from a reading incentive program like Accelerated Reader or Scholastic Reading Counts! (SRC), and not all books are on these lists.

If you determine that the request is for a book for fun and not specifically related to homework, there are several questions you can ask to help discover the child's reading interests.

Begin by asking if the child can recall a recent book he or she read for fun. If, for example, the answer is *Ramona* by Beverly Cleary, you can offer other books by that author. Or you can offer other humorous contemporary novels with a quirky girl main character, such as Barbara Park's *Junie B. Jones*, Megan McDonald's *Judy Moody*, or Paula Danziger's *Amber Brown*. The book the child mentions will also help you determine the child's reading level.

Next, ask what grade the child is in. This can help determine what the child can handle in the way of social issues and give an indication of reading level, but not always, because some children in the same grade read way below or way above that grade level. Also ask if the book is for that person, because some children visit the library to obtain books for a sibling. If you are dealing with the parent, you may want to ask if it is for a boy or girl, because sometimes gender plays a part in what type of books are requested, especially for children ages eight and above.

Readers' Advisory Questions

Following are some common questions you can use when doing the readers' advisory interview. Remember, you are not prying, or invading someone's privacy; you are just trying to determine what that person would enjoy in the way of recreational reading.

- ◆ What grade are you in?

- ◆ Is this for homework or to read for fun?

- ◆ Can you think of a book you read before? (for younger children)

- ◆ Can you think of a book you read and liked? (for 'tweens)

- ◆ Is this for you or for a brother or sister? (or for a child, if an adult is asking)

- ◆ Would you like something true (nonfiction) or a made-up story?

- Do you have a favorite book series?

- Do you have a favorite author?

- Do you like books that are scary or funny?

- Is there a hobby or sport you like?

- What movies and TV shows do you like?

Once you get some answers, you can start narrowing down the type of book that the young person might like. More detail about how to do that is provided below.

Body Language and Helpful Nonverbal Cues

The way you present yourself to the child or 'tween can make a big difference in how he or she responds to your questions. Many children are shy, or they have been taught not to bother an adult who looks busy. We have all had the unhappy experience of being waited on by a sales clerk who clearly seems too busy to want to help us; you do not want to convey that attitude when doing readers' advisory. Here are some non-verbal clues that can positively influence the exchange between you and a young person when doing the readers' advisory interview:

- Make eye contact.

- Smile.

- Listen with your full attention. Put away other work.

- Hold your arms and hands in a relaxed position (not crossed, no hands on hips).

- Be patient and unhurried.

- Provide several books to choose from.

- Walk away and let the person choose without pressure.

- Check back to see if additional suggestions are needed.

- When the person checks out, ask whether he or she enjoyed the books selected.

Finding Books for Children and 'Tweens

Once you have conducted the readers' advisory interview, there are several ways to find books for children and 'tweens. Often you can start by using the online catalog; if a 'tween asked for a novel and likes basketball, you can start by searching "basketball—fiction" or "basketball—juvenile fiction." The catalog can be a helpful tool in finding what the child is asking for, from picture books about trains for a preschooler, to vampire novels for the middle schooler who loved Stephenie Meyer's *Twilight* and would like something similar.

Another handy way to find books to recommend is to use handouts, such as "Great Books for Boys" and "Great Books for Girls." Paper handouts are an easy and useful way to help people find books; these handouts can be especially helpful to parents picking out books for their children who are not at the library with them. This book also explores other professional books, Web sites, and ways to find books for young readers.

Read-Alikes

If the 'tween is able to name a book he or she read in the past and enjoyed, try to find similar books. These are known as "read-alikes." If there is a regular request for certain titles or types of books, you may want to create handouts; for example, so many 'tweens finished the Harry Potter series and requested other books that were similar, that many libraries wrote up lists of other fantasy novels about kids with magical powers.

Finding Read-Alikes

If you discover the name of a book that the 'tween enjoyed, there are a few steps you can take to find something similar. One is to look at the genre: Was the book a mystery, adventure story, or humorous novel? Then you can find other books in that genre (there is more discussion of genre fiction in chapter 6).

Of course you may also offer other books by that same author. If a 'tween liked one Roald Dahl novel, it is likely he or she will enjoy his other books. Although some authors like Dahl don't write books in a series, many of their books have a similar style and elements that appeal to a reader.

Another simple way to find read-alikes is to use the library's online catalog. Look up the book mentioned as a favorite, and notice what subject headings are listed. See what other books are listed under the same subject headings.

Another method of finding read-alikes is to search on Amazon.com. If the 'tween really liked *Holes* by Louis Sachar, look up that book on Amazon. You will see the listing for the book, as well as other books that were purchased at the same time. These are not always read-alikes, but often they are similar books that will appeal to the same reader.

Using databases, such as NoveList, which are purchased by many libraries and available on their Web sites, can help you find read-alikes. Search for the book named by the 'tween as a favorite and see if there are links to other recommended reads. When I searched Sachar's *Holes* on NoveList, for example, I found a list of other novels about adventurous 'tweens, including Jerry Spinell's *Maniac Magee* and *Hoot* by Carl Hiaasen. Novelist also has "Grab and Go" booklists, which are other books with similar subject or genre headings that may appeal to the reader. Many databases provide lists of author read-alikes.

To create a list of read-alikes, search for other books in that genre, such as historical fiction, science fiction, or fantasy, or find other books with a similar main character, like an orphan or a young witch or wizard. Use the catalog to help you pinpoint these titles.

Quick Tips for Finding Books in a Hurry

Unfortunately, there may be times when you truly are too hurried to go through the usual readers' advisory steps, including the body language suggested above. Maybe the 'tween is there just a few minutes before the library's closing time. Or maybe the parent is outside honking the car horn, and the child needs a book right now or his mom will leave without him (this has happened to me more than once). Here are some tips for finding a book when you and the child only have a minute to choose something to read:

- ◆ Get away from the computer. Walk around and talk to young people and their caregivers.

- ◆ Look for what is popular, often on the hold shelves.

- ◆ Look for books that are repeatedly on the return shelves.

- ◆ Recommend books you have heard about in addition to books you have read.

- ◆ Display book jackets/covers; these often "sell" a book.

- ◆ Have handouts on good reads for boys and good reads for girls on hand.

- ◆ Have available handouts on "read-alikes," such as "If you like *Captain Underpants*, Try These!"

- ◆ If you have a "New" shelf in the children's area, look there.

Types of Books

Just like a salesperson at a bookstore, you, as the library staff person, should know something about the different categories in which children's books are shelved. That way, when offering readers' advisory, if the person wants a book about dogs, you can follow up by finding out what type of dog book: a nonfiction book on training a new puppy, a picture book for a very young child, an easy reader such as Norman Bridwell's Clifford series, a 'tween novel like *Shiloh* by Phyllis Reynolds Naylor, or a book of poetry about dogs. The categories of children's books found in most libraries include picture books, board books, easy readers, transitional fiction, fiction, nonfiction, graphic novels, and paperbacks. Each of these is discussed in detail in upcoming chapters.

It is important to find books for the appropriate reading and interest level of the child. Something too babyish or too difficult may turn off that reader. Offer lots of choices, because it can be difficult to discern a child's reading level; even if you know what grade a child is in, not all children in that grade read on the same level. If you offer a wide variety, the child can pick up books that are likely to be a good "fit."

Gender Issues

When kids get to be old enough to read novels on their own, they often want books with a boy main character if the reader is a boy, and a girl protagonist if the reader is a girl. Not all children react this way, and the book may be something both boys and girls want to read. The average boy does not want a book with a pink cover that has the word "princess" in the title, but many boys like the Ramona books by Beverly Cleary or Barbara Park's *Junie B. Jones*. So offer all types of books and let children figure out what works for them. If you are helping a parent who is seeking books for a fourth or fifth grader, ask whether it is a boy or girl, because that may help you offer more specific choices.

Bibliotherapy

At times parents may want a book for their children to help with the death of a grandparent, an impending divorce, or another issue. This is referred to as bibliotherapy. A book won't be the only counseling a child may need if his or her parents are divorcing, but books can help in the process or motivate a child to discuss the problem with a parent. Usually the online catalog can help you find books on these issues by searching under the subject and then looking for fiction on that subject.

Keeping Track of What You Read

When I first started as a librarian, we didn't have the Internet or computers, so I kept track of what I read with a little recipe card box. For each juvenile or teen novel I read, I filled out a card. Then when an older child asked for a book, I could look through my cards for books to suggest. Now there are free online versions of those file boxes! Following are three that I have tested; of course, on the Internet there are always changes and new things coming up. But these are popular and fairly standard, so they are worth exploring to see which suits your needs. Some libraries have in-house reading logs for staff and patrons, so check into that as well.

Goodreads. www.goodreads.com

Goodreads is similar to Shelfari, in that you keep a file of what you read and can share it with others. The site also runs an online book discussion club and has lists of favorites or "bests," such as "Best Young Adult Novels," or "Girl Power Books" that are perfect for 'tweens. Goodreads appears to be the most popular site of this type, especially with librarians, so you may find it suits your needs.

LibraryThing. www.librarything.com

Half a million people are members of LibraryThing, which is also a free online social networking site for sharing book suggestions. You can make your files using the data from Amazon.com or from the Library of Congress, so your online entries have complete bibliographic data. There are also many groups to join, if you have a special reading interest you want to share. For example, Teenage

Book Nudgers is a group of teens who love books, and offer suggestions for great reading. Check out what they recommend the next time a 'tween asks for something good to read.

Shelfari. www.shelfari.com

Shelfari is a social networking site that lets you build an online "bookcase," in which you can enter the books you have read and rate them. Then you can share your shelf with friends and view their online bookcases. If you work for a library system, encourage other library staff to join Shelfari, and you can share with each other.

Readers' Advisory Can Be Fun and Rewarding

Many of us went into the library profession because we loved books and reading. But that isn't always the case; maybe you like the library world because of computers or programs. You will still find readers' advisory a rewarding activity when you see the look on a child's face who found a book he or she loves. You may even feel like Santa Claus for a moment when that child comes in and thanks you for suggesting that book!

The next several chapters explore books you can recommend based on the child's age. Also included are some categories that are often overlooked when doing readers' advisory, such as folklore and poetry. Finally, the book concludes with some advice on promoting books to children and 'tweens.

Helpful Tools for Readers' Advisory

Until you have time to build your own knowledge of books, and before you have read many children's books yourself, it can be difficult to think of books even if you know the child you are helping likes mysteries, or fantasy, or realistic fiction. That is why you are reading this book, and the chapters contain lists of books by genre and by popularly requested topics. Following are a few professional books and Web sites that can help you find books to recommend, especially while you are still new to the readers' advisory process.

Print Guides

Barr, Catherine, and John T. Gillespie. *Best Books for Children: Preschool through Grade 6.* 9th ed. Westport, CT: Libraries Unlimited, 2010.

Organized thematically, more than 25,000 books are described and recommended for children in this handy reference book.

Lewis, Valerie V., and Walter M. Mayes. *Valerie and Walter's Best Books for Children: A Lively, Opinionated Guide— Revised and Updated.* New York: HarperCollins, 2004.

Two book experts offer thousands of reading recommendations for kids and teens, arranged by age level. The subject index is very detailed, and the annotations are often very funny and insightful.

Odean, Kathleen. *Great Books for Boys.* New York: Ballantine Books, 1998.

Odean, Kathleen. *Great Books for Girls.* New York: Ballantine Books, 2002.

Children's librarian Kathleen Odean is an expert in this field. She has published several guides to finding good books for children. In *Great Books for Boys,* she annotates more than 600 books recommended for boys, arranged by genre such as adventure, sports, and fantasy. *Great Books for Girls*, revised from her 1991 edition, offers hundreds of recreational reading suggestions aimed at girls.

Web Sites

Book Adventure Website. www.bookadventure.org

Book Adventure offers a great search tool to find books on almost any topic, and you can limit the search by grade level. Go to the Kids' Zone, then select Book Finder. Then choose fiction or nonfiction, pick a grade level, and pick up to five different topics, including genres such as adventure or humor, topics like animals or sports, or themes like friendship. The Web site also has quizzes teachers can use to reward reading comprehension. The Web site is sponsored by Sylvan Learning.

READ-ALIKES FOR
DIARY OF A WIMPY KID BY JEFF KINNEY

Amato, Mary. <u>Riot Brothers</u> series.

Benton, Jim. <u>Dear Dumb Diary</u> series.

Benton, Jim. *Franny K. Stein, Mad Scientist.*

Birdseye, Tom. *Attack of the Mutant Underwear.*

Child, Lauren. <u>Clarice Bean</u> chapter books.

Clement, Andrew. <u>Jake Drake</u> series.

Clement, Andrew. *Lunch Money.*

Codell, Esmé Raji. *Vive la Paris.*

Davis, Katie. *The Curse of Addy McMahon.*

Greenburg, Dan. <u>Zach Files</u> series.

Gutman, Dan. <u>My Weird School </u>series.

Haddix, Margaret Peterson. *Dexter the Tough.*

Haddix, Margaret Peterson. *Girl with 500 Middle Names.*

Holm, Jennifer L. <u>Babymouse</u> series.

Kerrin, Jessica Scott. <u>Martin Bridge</u> series.

McDonald, Megan. <u>Stink</u> series.

Moss, Marissa. <u>Amelia's Notebook</u> series.

Naylor, Phyllis Reynolds. *Roxie and the Hooligans.*

Paterson, Katherine. *The Field of the Dogs.*

Patneaude, David. *Colder Than Ice.*

Pennypacker, Sara. <u>Clementine</u> series.

Pilkey, Dav. <u>Captain Underpants</u> series.

Sachar, Louis. <u>Wayside School</u> series.

Spinelli, Jerry. *Wringer.*

Stauffacher, Sue. *Donuthead.*

Warner, Sally. *It's Only Temporary.*

Whybrow, Ian. <u>Little Wolf's Book of Badness</u> series.

Winkler, Henry. <u>Hank Zipzer</u> series.

READ-ALIKES FOR
THE WARRIORS SERIES BY ERIN HUNTER

Adams, Richard. *Watership Down.*

Avi. Poppy series.

Baldry, Cherith. Eaglesmount Trilogy.

Bell, Clare. The Named Ratha series.

Brooks, Walter R. Freddy the Pig series.

Carmody, Isobelle. *Little Fur: A Fox Called Sorrow.*

Fan, Nancy Yi. *Swordbird.*

Funke, Cornelia. *Dragonrider.*

George, Jean Craighead. *The Cats of Roxville Station.*

Hoeye, Michael. *Hermux Tantamoq Adventures.*

Iserles, Inbali. *The Tygrine Cat.*

Jacques, Brian. Redwall series.

Jansson, Tove. Moomintroll series.

Jarvis, Robin. The Deptford Mice series.

Lasky, Kathryn. Guardians of Ga'Hoole series.

Lisle, Janet Taylor. *Highway Cats.*

McAllister, Margaret. Mistmantle Chronicles.

Milway, Alex. *Mousehunter.*

Myers, Walter Dean. *Tree Swords for Granada.*

O'Brien, Robert. *Mrs. Frisby and the Rats of NIMH.*

Oppel, Kenneth. Silverwing series.

Pemberton, Bonnie. *The Cat Master.*

Petersen, David. *Mouse Guard.*

Pierce, Meredith Ann. Firebringer Trilogy.

Reiche, Dietlof. I, Freddy series.

Stratton, Gene. *Porter's Girl.*

Wallace, Bill. *The Legend of Thunderfoot.*

Westall, Robert. *Blitzcat.*

Westall, Robert. *Yaxley's Cat.*

Williams, Tad. *Tailchaser's Song.*

READ-ALIKES FOR THE
<u>PERCY JACKSON</u> SERIES BY RICK RIORDAN

Colfer, Eoin. *Artemis Fowl.*

Collins, Suzanne. <u>Gregor the Overlander</u> series.

Druitt, Tobias. *Corydon and the Island of Monsters.*

Farmer, Nancy. *Sea of Trolls.*

Funke, Cornelia. *Inkheart.*

Harris, Joanne. *Runemarks.*

Hennesy, Carolyn. *Pandora Gets Jealous.*

Kerr, Philip. *The Akhenaten Adventure.*

Landy, Derek. *Skulduggery Pleasant.*

Law, Ingrid. *Savvy.*

McMullan, Kate. *Have a Hot Time, Hades!*

Mull, Brandon. *Fablehaven.*

Sage, Angie. *Magyk.*

Scott, Michael. *The Alchemyst.*

Shipton, Paul. *The Pig Scrolls by Gryllus the Pig.*

Stewart, Trenton. *The Mysterious Benedict Society.*

Yolen, Jane. *Odysseus in the Serpent Maze.*

Chapter 2

Special Issues in Readers' Advisory for Children and 'Tweens

If you often work in readers' advisory, some issues and concerns will likely arise, and you should be prepared to deal with them. These issues can happen with all of the age groups addressed in the subsequent chapters. They are grouped below under various topics.

Trends and Popular Books for Children and 'Tweens

There are two distinct groups of books that are popular with children and 'tweens: great books (well written), and books based on TV shows or comic characters. 'Tweens often seek out well-written fiction, such as Newbery winners or best sellers by authors like J. K. Rowling, Rick Riordan, Jeff Kinney, Roald Dahl, and others. Look at what is on your hold and return shelves; you may find this to be true. Fortunately nearly all public and school libraries carry these popular books.

Fewer libraries carry the equally popular "junk food books," which include paperbacks based on TV series like *Hannah Montana* or comic character books like those starring Pokemon or Spongebob. Some school libraries have extremely small budgets, so it is understandable that they can't afford these, but they might be able to acquire them through donations or as the incentives for holding a book fair (many book fair vendors reward a library by donating books). Public libraries are also often on tight budgets, but they usually can afford a few of these books. We buy popular, mass market titles for adults, so why not for kids? If you are not sure what is currently popular, check the children's best-seller lists available from *Publishers Weekly* magazine (www.publishersweekly.com).

Assisting Reluctant Readers

Reluctant readers are children who read below grade level or just don't like reading even if they do read at grade level. Reluctant readers can be like picky eaters; they are more "choosy" about what they will read, so we have to help them find something they like. Perhaps the child has a learning disability. In that case, it is vital that we find something he or she *can* read, or the child may be turned off of reading forever.

Many reluctant readers are more inclined to look at magazines and comics, because the visual design is more inviting than a page of solid text. Some enjoy nonfiction and will read an informational book on a subject they are interested in, such as dinosaurs, cars and planes, or animals, especially if the book has great color photos. Find out what interests the reader and offer something on that topic: if the child is a video gamer, offer electronic gaming magazines. Some reluctant readers would rather read text on a computer screen than on a paper page, so we know they *can* read.

The readers' advisory interview with a reluctant reader generally takes more time, but once you find out a child's hobby or interest, you can usually get him or her to take a book or magazine on that topic.

If you have a very reluctant reader, there are a few things you can try to find a book that might appeal to that child:

- ◆ Check the best-seller lists.

- ◆ Look at what is on the return shelf.

- ◆ Look at what is regularly on the hold shelf.

- ◆ Take the child to the children's paperbacks section; series books often appeal to reluctant readers.

- Find novelty books like *Egyptology* or *Pirateology*: books with pop-ups, foldouts, and other three-dimensional characteristics.

- Find nonfiction books filled with photos on the child's favorite hobby.

- Offer a book based on the child's favorite TV shows.

- Find humorous books, such as Dav Pilkey's <u>Captain Underpants</u> series.

- Offer a book based on a movie.

During the readers' advisory interview, you might find that the child just doesn't express any interest in books. Try asking if he or she has a favorite TV show or movie; many children's movies are based on books, from the recent *Tale of Despereaux* to *Charlie and the Chocolate Factory*. And many popular children's TV series, often those found on the Disney channel or Nickelodeon, have been turned into paperback books. For a list of children's movies found in book form, visit en.wikipedia. org/wiki/List_of_children's_books_made_into_feature_films.

Another strategy is to try paperback series books; these often appeal to a reluctant reader. Just take the child over to the shelves and let him or her explore alone. To find out the order of books in a series, visit www. mcpl.lib.mo.us/readers/series/juv/.

Books for Boys

There is a growing concern among educators that boys stop reading around the fourth grade, when more of their free time is taken up with team sports, video games, and other activities. On the other hand, many boys this age read lengthy books like the <u>Harry Potter</u> series, so what is really happening?

Part of the problem is that some boys say libraries don't have enough of what they want to read, which includes comic books and graphic novels, paperback series books, and other books not considered "literature." They like to read magazines, and read things on Web sites, but just don't like novels. So, if you are dealing with a boy who just doesn't seem interested in what you are suggesting, try some of the following:

- Offer nonfiction with lots of photos on a subject he is interested in.

- Offer books based on TV show or movies.

- ◆ Offer comic books.

- ◆ Offer magazines.

- ◆ Offer joke and riddle books.

- ◆ Offer books of "lists" like *The Guinness Book of World Records.*

- ◆ Offer books on "gross" things like insects, grossology, and monsters.

- ◆ Try books listed on www.guysread.com/ or www.richiespicks. com.

Jon Scieszka, a popular children's author, former teacher, and former National Ambassador for Young People's Literature for the Library of Congress, has been a major advocate for helping librarians and teachers offer boys books they would like to read. Guys Read is his project; check out www.guysread.com. He believes boys will read if we let them choose their own books and don't belittle their choices, whether *MAD Magazine*, a Spongebob joke book, or a coffee-table book on World War II.

Richie Parthington is a dad and youth services librarian, who maintains a Web site suggesting great books for 'tweens and teens. Many of his favorites appeal to boys (and girls, too). Check out his suggestions at www.richiespicks.com.

A great reference book on helping boys find books in the library is *Best Books for Boys* by Matthew D. Zbaracki. It is arranged by type of book, such as picture books and novels, and there is a very detailed subject index. If you are a newer children's librarian or new to doing readers' advisory with boys, it can be really helpful.

Promote Books to Girls, Too

Although it is important to help boys find books they will enjoy reading, girls should not be neglected. Be sure you have displays, programs, and books that girls are requesting, from "princess" books to novels featuring female protagonists. Remember, dismissing the novels 'tween girls enjoy as "chick lit" is sexist and unfair. Having books that all children, boys and girls alike, enjoy is key to being a successful readers' advisor. At the end of this chapter are lists of books to recommend to boys and girls. These may be copied to give to parents who are picking out books for their 'tweens who are not at the library.

Assisting Young English Language Learners

You may encounter children and 'tweens who are in the process of learning English and would like books to read. Sometimes they want books in their native languages, such as Spanish or Chinese. If there is a large enough population in your area who read in that language, it is worth the money to carry some books for that audience. If not, you can try to obtain some through interlibrary loan, or direct children to a nearby library that carries the materials they are requesting.

English language learners also want books in English, but may not yet read at their grade levels. Find them nonfiction that contains abundant photographs and other illustrative material that will help them decode what the text is saying. These will be helpful for homework assignments as well as recreational reading. Many children and 'tweens who are learning English enjoy graphic novels and comic books, because the illustrations help them figure out what the text says. Also provide recorded books, so they can read along and practice English pronunciation. Luckily, there is a wide selection of both picture books that have an accompanying CD, and popular 'tween novels on CD. Find a paper copy of the novel to go along with the recorded book. More libraries are stocking Playaways and other MP3 versions of recorded books that appeal to 'tweens.

Censorship Challenges

Sometimes parents have objections to a book that you recommend to their young children, 'tweens, or even teens. So let's briefly discuss what to do when a parent objects to a book.

The success of <u>Harry Potter</u> has caused some who are deeply religious to object to what they see as the book's "sorcery" elements. It is not that they believe the book is for an older child; it is the topic of "witchcraft" that they object to for any age group. If that is the case, you can find books that are not fantasy. Look for "classics" like *Little Women, Little House on the Prairie*, or Fitzgerald's <u>The Great Brain</u> series, because these families tend to like traditional books.

If the parents object to a book's content due to sex and cursing, it could be that they feel the book is fine for an older teen, but not for their middle schooler. If that is the case, try offering some Newbery winners or honor books; parents often have heard of the Newbery award and understand these are books recommended as great literature.

When parents object to a book, be sure to give them a copy of the library's policy on selection or a "reconsideration" form if they want the library to get rid of the book. Often parents just want someone to listen to the complaint, but won't ask for any action to be taken. Parents may just want different choices for their child, but don't expect you to "ban" the book. A great "tool" to have before a parent objects to a book is the Intellectual Freedom "first aid kit," available from the American Library Association (www.ala.org/ala/aboutala/offices/oif/iftoolkits/intellectual.cfm). Look this over before you get a complaint so you have a strategy ready in case you receive a challenge to a book. Most libraries have a policy on censorship and book challenges; familiarize yourself with it so you can adhere to it when the time comes.

Helping Teachers Find Books for the Classroom

Assisting teachers in finding books for their classrooms can be a very rewarding experience, especially when you can collaborate with the teacher. If you think about it, helping a teacher means you are helping the twenty to thirty students in that classroom! But helping a teacher after school, when the library is packed with people, can be a challenge. So encourage teachers to phone or e-mail their requests ahead of time, to be picked up later. Think of it as a "to go" order; if the teacher calls ahead, the books can be ready for pickup when he or she gets to the library.

When a teacher calls, conduct the same type of interview you would with an in-person request—how many books, what is the subject, is he or she looking for read-alouds, or one book per student on the subject? Once you know what the teacher wants, you can pull the books in the morning (or whenever it is not busy), and then the teacher can pick up the box and check the books out. I have found that teachers appreciate this service so much they are easily convinced to phone or e-mail ahead of time.

If a teacher is there in person on a busy afternoon, of course you can still help. Get the teacher started using the catalog, and come back and check on him or her periodically. When a teacher is checking out nonfiction for the class to use for a project, suggest a few short read-alouds that would be great to kick off the lesson. For example, Scieszka and Smith's *Science Verse*, a collection of illustrated humorous poems, is a great book to use at the beginning of a science lesson. There are many great picture books for older readers that touch on historical subjects; they work great for a read-aloud that coincides with a social studies lesson. For example, Patrcia Polacco's *Pink and Say* is brief enough to read in one sitting to a fifth-grade class learning about slavery and the U.S. Civil War, but the teacher may not ask specifically for that book when picking up Civil War nonfiction. So try to tuck in a few related poetry or story read-alouds when a teacher needs nonfiction on a specific topic.

Helpful Electronic Sources on Special Issues

When I first started as a children's librarian, there were very few reference books to help with readers' advisory. I read nearly all of the new children's books that the library bought so I would know what books to recommend. Now there are several great Web sites and subscription databases to help locate books for 'tweens, especially helpful for staff members who are not full-time children's librarians.

Web Sites

Children's Books Made into Films. en.wikipedia.org/wiki/List_of_children's_books_made_into_feature_films

If you're dealing with a 'tween or teen who doesn't seem interested in anything but needs to get a book, suggest one that has been made into a movie. These books will often appeal to reluctant readers.

Children's Paperback Series Books. www.mcpl.lib.mo.us/readers/series/juv/

If a child, 'tween, or teen likes series books, this Web site can help you find out the order in which books have been published in a series.

Guys Read. www.guysread.com

Award-winning author Jon Scieszka, who used to be a second-grade teacher, has this Web site that lists great books to recommend to boys. Many educators see a gender divide in reading: boys read less than girls, and often don't read at grade level to a greater degree than girls. Guys Read also has advice for librarians, teachers, and parents on getting boys interested in books.

Intellectual Freedom Toolkit. www.ala.org/ala/aboutala/offices/oif/iftoolkits/intellectual.cfm

From the American Library Association's Office of Intellectual Freedom, this online toolkit offers forms and details procedures for dealing with challenges to library books by parents and others.

Richie's Picks. http://www.richiespicks.com

An easy-to-search Web site maintained by youth services librarian Richie Parthington; most of his favorites will appeal to boys (as well as girls).

Databases

Most public libraries subscribe to databases of newspaper and magazine articles, and other online resources that are not "free"; they look like Web sites but require the user to enter your library card number to access them. One popular database was *What Do I Read Next?* But Gale, the company that provides it, updated this service and is now calling it *Books and Authors.* Although it has books for children and 'tweens, it isn't aimed at that audience, and as of this writing is still in the developmental stage, so it is not available for a full review. But there are two available databases on readers' advisory for youth:

Children's Literature Database (CLCD)

Unlike NovelList, which is designed for use by the library customer, the Children's Literature Database (often called CLCD) is aimed at the librarian or teacher. But it is very handy to use, listing lots of books, along with reviews of those books. You can search for a specific book or for award-winning titles. You can also find reading lists by grade level, and use other search methods to find books on similar subjects.

NoveList and NoveList K–8 Plus

The most prominent readers' advisory database, NoveList was originally designed to recommend books to adults. This new version for grades K–8 recently received an "A+" from *School Library Journal,* the highest rating possible. NoveList is very easy to use; enter the age group (younger children, older kids, teens, or adults) and describe elements of a plot or look for a type of book (mystery, fantasy, etc.). You can search by plot elements if the patron is asking for a book but can't remember the title. Or you can click on the various lists of popular books, award winners, and seasonal topics like Black History Month. The database is updated regularly, and in most libraries it is linked to the catalog so you can find a suggestion and click on it, to see if it is in your library. In my experience, 'tweens and teens like to use it themselves once you show it to them, because it is fun to enter different subjects and just click around the database.

BOOKS BOYS ENJOY

Books for Boys of All Ages

Black, Michael Ian. *Chicken Cheeks.*

Evans, Cambria. *Bone Soup.*

Fenton, Joe. *What's Under the Bed?*

Gravett, Emily. *Little Mouse's Big Book of Fears.*

Greven, Alec. *How to Talk to Girls.*

Harrison, Joanna. *Grizzly Dad.*

Hillman, Ben. *How Fast Is It? A Zippy Book All About Speed.*

Hillman, Ben. *How Weird Is It? A Freaky Book All About Strangeness.*

Various. *Zany Miscellany: A Mixed-Up Encyclopedia of Fun Facts!*

Books for Younger Boys, Ages Three to Eight

Arnold, Tedd. <u>Fly Guy</u> series.

Brown, Marc. <u>Arthur</u> series.

Burton, Virginia Lee. *Mike Mulligan and His Steam Shovel.*

Cosby, Bill. <u>Little Bill</u> series.

Feiffer, Jules. *Meanwhile . . .*

Johnson, Crockett. *Harold and the Purple Crayon.*

London, Jonathan. <u>Froggy</u> series.

Long, Melinda. *Pirates Don't Change Diapers.*

Marshall, James. <u>Fox</u> series.

Mills, Claudia. <u>Gus and Grandpa</u> series.

Pilkey, Dav. *Dog Breath!*

Pinkney, Brian. *Max Found Two Sticks.*

Rey, H. A., and Margret Rey. *Curious George.*

Sendak, Maurice. *Where the Wild Things Are.*

Shannon, David. <u>No, David</u> series.

Sharmat, Marjorie. <u>Nate the Great</u> series.

Willems, Mo. <u>Elephant and Piggie</u> series.

Yolen, Jane. <u>Commander Toad</u> series.

Zimmerman, Andrea. *Trashy Town.*

Books for 'Tween Boys, Ages Eight to Twelve

Barry, Dave. *Peter and the Starcatchers.*

Collins, Suzanne. <u>Gregor the Overlander</u> series.

Dahl, Roald. *Danny, the Champion of the World.*

Gantos, Jack. <u>Joey Pigza</u> series.

Jacques, Brian. <u>Redwall</u> series.

Juster, Norton. *The Phantom Tollbooth.*

Kinney, Jeff. <u>Diary of a Wimpy Kid</u> series.

Paolini, Christopher. <u>Eragon</u> series.

Pilkey, Dav. <u>Captain Underpants</u> series.

Riordan, Rick. <u>Percy Jackson</u> series.

Sachar, Louis. *Holes.*

Scieszka, Jon. <u>Time Warp Trio</u> series.

BOOKS GIRLS ENJOY

Books for Younger Girls, Ages Three to Eight

Byars, Betsy. <u>The Golly Sisters</u> series.

Cazet, Denys. *Minnie and Moo.*

DiCamillo, Kate. <u>Mercy Watson</u> series.

Falconer, Ian. <u>Olivia</u> series.

Guest, Elissa Haden. *Iris and Walter.*

Hoffman, Mary. *Amazing Grace.*

Holabird, Katherine. <u>Angelina Ballerina</u> series.

Kann, Victoria. *Pinkalicious.*

Meddaugh, Susan. <u>Martha</u> series.

O'Connor, Jane. <u>Fancy Nancy</u> series.

Rylant, Cynthia. <u>Mr. Putter and Tabby</u> series.

Books for 'Tween Girls, Ages Eight to Twelve

Barrows, Annie. <u>Ivy and Bean</u> series.

Birdsall, Jeanne. *The Penderwicks.*

Blume, Judy. *Are You There, God? It's Me, Margaret.*

Byars, Betsy. <u>Herculeah Jones</u> series.

Cushman, Karen. *Midwife's Apprentice.*

Danziger, Paula. <u>Amber Brown</u> series.

Holm, Jennifer L. <u>Babymouse</u> series.

Lowry, Lois. *Number the Stars.*

McDonald, Megan. <u>Judy Moody</u> series.

Spinelli, Eileen. *Summerhouse Time.*

Van Draanen, Wendelin. <u>Sammy Keyes</u> series.

Wiles, Deborah. *Love, Ruby Lavender.*

NOVELS FOR FAMILIES WANTING
TRADITIONAL BOOKS

Alcott, Louisa May. *Little Women.*

Atwater, Richard, and Florence Atwater. *Mr. Popper's Penguins.*

Birdsall, Jeanne. <u>The Penderwicks</u> series.

Birney, Betty G. *The Seven Wonders of Sassafras Springs.*

Brink, Carol Ryrie. *Caddie Woodlawn.*

Burnett, Frances Hodgson. *A Little Princess.*

Burnett, Frances Hodgson. *The Secret Garden.*

Burnford, Sheila. *Incredible Journey.*

Butterworth, Oliver. *The Enormous Egg.*

Cleary, Beverly. <u>Beezus and Ramona</u> series.

Estes, Eleanor. <u>The Moffats</u> series.

Farley, Walter. <u>Black Stallion</u> series.

Fitzgerald, John D. <u>The Great Brain</u> series.

Forbes, Esther. *Johnny Tremain.*

Harlow, Joan Hiatt. *Thunder from the Sea.*

Knight, Eric. *Lassie Come Home.*

Lenski, Lois. <u>Strawberry Girl</u> series.

Lovelace, Maud Hart. <u>Betsy Tacy</u> series.

McCloskey, Robert. *Homer Price.*

Milne, A. A. <u>Winnie the Pooh</u> series.

Montgomery, L. M. <u>Anne of Green Gables</u> series.

Robertson, Keith. <u>Henry Reed</u> series.

Wilder, Laura Ingalls. <u>Little House</u> series.

'TWEEN NOVELS MADE INTO POPULAR FILMS

Alcott, Louisa May. *Little Women.*

Alexander, Lloyd. *The Black Cauldron.*

Babbitt, Natalie. *Tuck Evelasting.*

Baum, L. Frank. *The Wizard of Oz.*

Black, Holly. *The Spiderwick Chronicles.*

Burnett, Frances Hodgson. *The Secret Garden.*

Burnford, Sheila. *The Incredible Journey.*

Cabot, Meg. *The Princess Diaries.*

Carroll, Lewis. *Alice in Wonderland.*

Cooper, Susan. *The Dark Is Rising.*

Dahl, Roald. *Charlie and the Chocolate Factory.*

Dahl, Roald. *James and the Giant Peach.*

Dahl, Roald. *Matilda.*

Dahl, Roald. *The Witches.*

DiCamillo, Kate. *Because of Winn Dixie.*

DiCamillo, Kate. *Tale of Despereaux.*

DuPrau, Jeanne. *The City of Ember.*

Farley, Walter. *The Black Stallion.*

Fine, Anne. *Alias Madame Doubtfire.*

Fitzhugh, Louise. *Harriet the Spy.*

Fleming, Ian. *Chitty Chitty Bang Bang.*

Funke, Cornelia. *Inkheart.*

Gaiman, Neil. *Coraline.*

Gipson, Fred. *Old Yeller.*

Hiaasen, Carl. *Hoot.*

Hoffman, Alice. *Aquamarine.*

Horowitz, Anthony. *Stormbreaker.*

King-Smith, Dick. *Babe the Pig.*

King-Smith, Dick. *The Water Horse.*

Konigsburg, E. L. *From the Mixed-Up Files of Mrs. Basil E. Frankweiler.*

L'Engle, Madeleine. *A Wrinkle in Time.*

Levine, Gail Carson. *Ella Enchanted.*

Lewis, C. S. *The Chronicles of Narnia: The Lion, the Witch, and the Wardrobe.*

Lewis, C. S. *Prince Caspian.*

Lindgren, Astrid. *Pippi Longstocking.*

Montgomery, Lucy Maud. *Anne of Green Gables.*

O'Dell, Scott. *Island of the Blue Dolphins.*

Orr, Wendy. *Nim's Island.*

Paolini, Christopher. *Eragon.*

Paterson, Katherine. *Bridge to Terabithia.*

Paulsen, Gary. *Hatchet* (film: *A Cry in the Wilderness*).

Pullman, Philip. *The Golden Compass.*

Raskin, Ellen. *The Westing Game* (film: *Get a Clue*).

Rawls, Wilson. *Where the Red Fern Grows.*

Rockwell, Thomas. *How to Eat Fried Worms.*

Rodgers, Mary. *Freaky Friday.*

Rowling, J. K. <u>Harry Potter</u> series.

Sachar, Louis. *Holes.*

Smith, Dodie. *The Hundred and One Dalmatians* (film: *101 Dalmatians*).

Snicket, Lemony. *A Series of Unfortunate Events.*

Travers, P. L. *Mary Poppins.*

Tripp, Valerie. *Kit Kittredge: American Girl.*

White, E. B. *Charlotte's Web.*

White, E. B. *Stuart Little.*

Chapter 3

Readers' Advisory for Young Children Ages Birth to Five

Young children (babies, toddlers, and preschoolers) often visit the library weekly, either for storytime or for something to do. There is a great deal of emphasis in our media on parents reading to young children so they will be ready to learn when they get to kindergarten. So there are often preschoolers in the library with a parent or caregiver, looking for books to check out. They can be one of the largest groups of library users, so this chapter explores how to help them find books they will enjoy.

Determining a Young Child's Interests

Even when I was a new librarian, I found it easier to find a book for a preschooler than for a middle schooler. Preschoolers often want books on a certain topic, but are willing to try other books, too. In spite of their flexibility, you should still do the readers' advisory interview. Preschoolers do have certain interests and deserve books on those topics as well as the books all preschoolers need to read before starting kindergarten (which are listed at the end of this chapter). After you have asked the questions discussed in the first chapter, use the online catalog to find the topic, such as "Princesses—juvenile fiction," and walk over to the picture book area to see what is available. Show the covers; these are often enough to help the child decide that book is of interest. The following section discusses what types of books are aimed at young children—books you read to children before they can read on their own.

Types of Books for Young Children

Picture books are the largest group of books for young children, but there are a few other types of books you can offer parents to read to children as well. Not all libraries circulate all of these types of books, but this will give you a general idea of what is published for children from birth to age five.

Board Books

Board books are usually small, handheld cardboard books of approximately eight to twelve pages in length, intended for babies. They can hold up to a toddler's grip, and often have very simple photographs or cartoon illustrations and very little text. Some of the best are the Max the bunny board books, created by Rosemary Wells; they have now evolved into longer picture books starring Max and his bossy sister Ruby. But the original Max books are pithy, humorous board books, in which Max often spoke in one-word sentences. Another award-winning picture book author/illustrator who has created great board books is Kevin Henkes (*Julius's Candy Corn* and *Sheila Rae's Peppermint Stick*); his are the standard twelve pages in length and tell simple, funny stories that have a beginning, middle, and end. My favorite board books are those by Sandra Boynton; they are hilarious to an adult, but also very baby/toddler appropriate. They contain cartoonlike illustrations and have funny, brief stories.

Currently there is a trend to turn popular picture books into board books. This is not usually successful. The shrunken illustrations lose too much detail, or the text is abridged; it is usually better to find board books that started as board books and are not just "dumbed down" picture books. Bill Martin's *Chicka Chicka Boom Boom* originated as a picture book; the board book version chopped off the ending to fit in the smaller format!

Not all libraries carry board books, although it is becoming more acceptable to circulate them. They can be shelved in bins, in tubs, or on shelves; be sure they are within reach of a toddler. They are relatively inexpensive, so if they wear out after a few years, they can be replaced without spending a lot of money.

Pop-up or Toy Books

Many libraries find it difficult to carry pop-up books because they don't hold up to circulation. Sometimes you can purchase a few pop-up books to be used in the library only, like toys owned by the library that don't circulate but are popular at the library. Or you might purchase a pop-up book just to use at storytimes. One series that does hold up to library usage and circulation is Eric Hill's <u>Spot</u>, about a yellow dog. These simple, sweet stories appeal to toddlers, and the flaps, which can be lifted to reveal a hidden picture, are relatively sturdy. One of the first "toy" books was *Pat the Bunny* by Dorothy Kunhardt; it has tactile fur, cloth, and other interactive elements and has been a best seller since it debuted in 1940!

Wordless Books

Just because a book has no words doesn't mean it is for babies and toddlers. Many wordless books are quite sophisticated, especially those by Caldecott medalist David Wiesner (*Tuesday*, *Flotsam*, and *Sector 7*). A wordless book that is very popular with young children is Peggy Rathmann's *Good Night Gorilla*; the illustrations clearly depict a story about a zoo. Children "read" the pictures and can narrate the story; this type of book works especially well one-on-one and to help children who cannot read a text yet but can read the pictures. Teachers also use these for writing exercises for school-aged children. One of the most popular is *Changes, Changes* by Pat Hutchins, which appeals to a wide age range.

Picture Books

Many see the primary goal of read-aloud picture books for preschoolers as instilling the love of books, literature, and reading in children, so that they will grow up to be lifelong readers. Picture books are intended for an adult to read to a child; most have texts that are not "easy to read," but contain rich vocabulary, dialogue, and texts, as well as illustrations that can be seen from a distance and "tell" a great deal of the story. Generally, picture books are larger in size than easy readers and novels; they are almost skinny versions of coffee-table books, often 32 pages in length. Some are small, handheld books like those by Beatrix Potter, but the majority are larger than 8½ by 11 inches.

Narrative Story Picture Books

Picture books include wordless books, concept books, or a rhyme, but most are basically short, fictional stories. Think of those from your own childhoods—*Madeline* by Ludwig Bemelmans, or *Where the Wild Things Are* by Maurice Sendak. These tell a story with a beginning, middle, and end. They have memorable, original characters. Often they show a small child overcoming adversity or standing up to be the hero; these are very appealing for preschoolers, who often feel powerless. Some of these stories have just one sentence per page, some a whole paragraph, but if the story line is strong, preschoolers will listen to a story that is more than five minutes in length (of read-aloud time). Humor is often successful with this age group, but sad stories can also be popular if they are not overly manipulative or didactic (such as those with a heavy-handed message). Picture books are dependent on both the text and illustration working together to tell the story; there are some authors who are also the illustrator, but that is not that common. Most books are created when a text is purchased and the editor or publisher sends it to an illustrator for the pictures; sometimes the author and illustrator don't even meet! "Picture book" is a format; not all picture books are for children ages four and younger, but for the most part, children in the birth to age four group enjoy picture books more than other types of books (novels, nonfiction, etc.).

Concept Books

A specialized type of picture book is the concept book, which demonstrates such concepts as colors, shapes, the alphabet, opposites, and numbers and counting. These can be as simple as a book with one word captioning a picture or photo that demonstrates the concept, or a book that conveys a story while demonstrating the concept at the same time. Concept books are some of the most popular picture books and are essential to library collections. Many kindergarten readiness lists remind parents that children need to know these concepts before they enter kindergarten.

The simplest concept books demonstrate a concept; for example, Tana Hoban's *Red, Blue, Yellow Shoe* is basically made up of captioned photos. Others, like Bill Martin's *Brown Bear, Brown Bear, What Do You See?* give examples of basic colors, but also tell a story and have a rhyming pattern. Both types of books are important; the simple concept books clearly depict the theme, whereas the more multileveled concept books tell a story, involve the audience, and reinforce a concept that may already be familiar. Sometimes more than one concept is explored, as in the alphabet book that also involves counting, or a concept book that has a theme and provides more information than just the concept. Lois Ehlert's *Eating the Alphabet* names several fruits and vegetables for each letter of the alphabet.

Alphabet Books

Some of the earliest picture books were alphabet books; Kate Greenaway's *A Apple Pie* and Edward Lear's *An Edward Lear Alphabet Book* were both published more than 100 years ago. Alphabet books are still published in abundance; too often they are created just to show off the artwork and are not really aimed at the preschooler who is learning the alphabet. Sometimes the alphabet is just the organizational device for a nonfiction book for older children; think of the entertaining books on the states that list an item for each letter of the alphabet for each state. These are better for fifth graders doing state reports than for preschoolers (e.g., *G Is for Golden: A California Alphabet* by David Dominiconi).

Alphabet books can sometimes have a plot that actually tells a story. Joseph Slate's *Miss Bindergarten Gets Ready for Kindergarten* and the sequels are about a class of twenty-six children, all animals with first names that depict the alphabet, and contain a story that describes what it is like to go to school.

Counting Books

Counting books are also published in great numbers (pardon the pun); sometimes they just serve the artist, but they can also be quite helpful in teaching counting and numbers. One of my pet peeves is a counting book that only depicts the word for the number and items to count, but doesn't include the numeral! I find it best if a counting book shows both the word *and* numeral, and has the appropriate number of items to count. There are many great counting songs ("This Old Man" and "Over in the Meadow") that work well as picture books for counting.

Colors and Shapes

Colors, opposites, and shapes are also important subjects in concept picture books. It is my experience that there are many great books on the colors, but far fewer on shapes or opposites, and these topics are very important for preschoolers to learn for kindergarten readiness. *Mouse Paint* by Ellen Walsh has a fun story, but also shows how primary colors are mixed to obtain secondary colors. Bill Martin's series of books that started with *Brown Bear, Brown Bear, What Do You See?* are really effective at teaching colors.

Multicultural Concept Books

Concept books can also explore or celebrate the concept through a culture. Roseanne Thong's *Round Is a Mooncake* and *Red Is a Dragon* introduce objects from Asian American culture. *Jambo Means Hello* and *Moja Means One* by Tom Feelings and Muriel Feelings are set in Africa (in Kenya) and use Swahili words.

In some ways, concept books are the first nonfiction books a child sees. Often even young children will grasp the idea that something in a photo is "real," and artwork means the book is "made up," so using concept books with photos can be really effective as a teaching tool. There is more on nonfiction for young children in chapter 8.

Mother Goose and Nursery Rhymes

Nursery rhymes are common throughout the world; in Western culture, they became known as Mother Goose rhymes around 1760. Some think Mother Goose was based on the English monarch Elizabeth I. These rhymes, in whatever language, appeal to babies and toddlers for many reasons. They are bouncy, and songlike, and music has a great effect on a baby. The rhymes often have alliteration, and some even have tongue twisters. They feature animals and humor—two topics of great appeal to toddlers. They often involve counting or the alphabet. They are as catchy as advertising jingles, are as memorable as TV theme songs, and can build an immediate connection between a baby and a caregiver.

Two older versions of Mother Goose rhymes and illustrations are still popular—Kate Greenaway's and Arthur Rackham's illustrations are still in print in Mother Goose collections. They were originally done about 150 years ago. Scholars Peter Opie and Ione Opie compiled several Mother Goose and nursery rhyme collections that are still in print. Randolph Caldecott, for whom the children's book illustration award is named, published *Hey Diddle Diddle Picture Book* in the late 1880s. The two major differences between Mother Goose collections are the illustrations and the choice of rhymes that are included. Those two factors will influence what choices you make to offer a parent asking for Mother Goose books.

The best-selling contemporary Mother Goose collections are those illustrated by Rosemary Wells; these have a wide age appeal, from babies to even emergent readers. The bright colors and animal characters are very eye-catching. A few years ago, the equally charming illustrated Mother Goose by Tomie DePaola had many of the same qualities—bright colors and animal characters. First published in 1968, Robert Wyndham's *Chinese Mother Goose Rhymes*, illustrated in soft watercolors by Ed Young, is still popular in parts of the United States where many residents speak and read Chinese. There are now some bilingual English/Spanish nursery rhyme books, such as *Tortillas Para Mama*, which have the same appeal as Mother Goose rhymes. Or try *Pio Peep: Traditional Spanish Nursery Rhymes* by Alma Flor Ada.

All of these are "gateway" books, leading young children to the love of rhyme and poetry. Mother Goose should be the starting, not stopping, point for this audience to experience rhyming texts. Once they are preschoolers who can recite Mother Goose rhymes from memory (an important kindergarten readiness skill), you can follow up with poetry collections for young children. There is more on poetry books in chapter 10.

Assisting Parents

When you are assisting teens and 'tweens, you have the advantage of working with them face-to-face and hearing from them about their reading tastes and information/homework needs. But for children under the age of eight, librarians often work with the parents and teachers to find books to be read out loud, either as bedtime stories or to the preschool class or daycare group. So learning to work with parents and teachers is an essential skill for library staff serving preschoolers.

Of course, librarians do serve children directly in programs like storytime, but after that, when a child and caregiver want to check out books to read at home, librarians often help the caregiver choose the books. Even if the child is asking for "train books," the readers' advisor has to interview the adult to figure out if that means nonfiction books with photographs of trains, or stories about trains, or specifically Thomas the Tank engine books, and what books the child may already have at home or may have read several times. So our interactions with parents and teachers are very important.

Readers' Advisory Interview with Parents

Many studies show that reading aloud to a child on a daily basis by a parent or caregiver is the one best way to "grow" a reader. Perhaps that parent cannot come to the library's storytime, but will come to check out books to read at home. If that happens, conduct an interview to help the parent pick out age-appropriate picture books and other materials. Asking about children's ages during your readers' advisory interview can help the parent understand that the one-year-old may need board books and very easy stories, and older preschoolers need books to help them get ready for kindergarten, like counting and alphabet books, along with good stories. Maybe the parent doesn't even realize the baby needs books and is at first just picking out books for the four-year-old. Have handouts aimed at these parents, or put out a monthly newsletter announcing the new books and media for preschoolers, recommended read-alouds for babies, your choices for the best books for toddlers, or books for those needing recommendations for gift books for this age group.

When to Include the Child

Many librarians were trained to include the child and parent together in the readers' advisory interview. This can also be applied to families with preschoolers. I try to include both; the parents can be very helpful in explaining what they want, but this "empowers" the child to be included in the conversation. You and dad may find lots of great train picture book stories, but the child can tell you that he has heard that one a "million times" at daycare, and may want something else. Or the preschooler may have asked for train books, but really wants only Thomas the Tank Engine stories. Or she may be open to trying picture books about machines other than trains, including stories about cars, boats, planes, steam shovels, etc.

When Not to Include the Child

There may be times when a parent needs to speak to you without the child hearing; for example, mom may want a book about the death of a pet, because she needs to prepare her child for that sad event, which may occur in the near future. Or the parent needs a preschool-level book or story about divorce, the death of a grandparent, moving to a new town, or another sensitive subject. Let the parent talk to you, and then you can decide if it is appropriate to include the child in the conversation. This can also give you the opportunity to let the parent know about adult-level books on the same topic or books from the parenting shelf on how to deal with a sensitive situation; the parent may not even be aware the library has a parenting shelf. The parents' shelf in your children's section of the library may hold books on baby care, nutrition, dealing with schools, and other types of parenting books.

Caregivers and Teachers

Another key audience for library staff who serve young children are the daycare providers, preschool teachers, nannies, babysitters, and other caregivers. They are looking for things to do with the children and will appreciate help in finding books. Many daycares and preschools have circle time, very similar to library storytime; the teachers appreciate help in pulling books for that week or having themed "kits" with books and materials. I encourage teachers, including preschool and daycare teachers, to phone ahead and let me know the "theme" of the week, so I can pull lots of great picture books on apples, bears, cats, days of the week, or whatever the theme is. Ask some of the same readers' advisory questions you would use with a parent: How old are these young children—are they toddlers, or preschoolers just about to enter kindergarten? The answer can help you in choosing the appropriate books for that daycare or preschool group.

Picture Books Can Be the Start of Lifelong Reading

For those who conduct library storytimes, picture books are the easiest type of book to recommend during readers' advisory, since they have read so many to storytime audiences. But for newer library staff members or those who do not conduct storytimes, it can be a big category to learn about. Browse the picture book shelves and see which authors have published multiple titles, such as Eric Carle. Also, look at the return shelves to see which picture books are regularly checked out, so you can learn what is popular and recommend these to others. Many adults can still name their favorite picture books from childhood, from Sendak's *Where the Wild Things Are* to Carle's *The Very Hungry Caterpillar*; popular picture books will be best sellers for decades. Once preschoolers find favorite books, hopefully they are hooked on the reading habit and will continue to be when they learn to read on their own.

Helpful Books and Web Sites on Books for Young Children

Of course, you will use your online library catalog, and search "Trains—Juvenile Fiction," or whatever the topic is, when the family is requesting picture books on a certain topic. But there are several great Web sites and reference books that can help you find lots of books for young children, for the parent or caregiver to use as read-alouds.

Caldecott Medal Books. www.ala.org/ala/mgrps/divs/alsc/ awardsgrants/bookmedia/caldecottmedal/aboutcaldecott/ aboutcaldecott.cfm

A list of the Caldecott Medal award-winning books for illustrations, given by the Association of Library Service to Children, a division of the American Library Association. Most of these are great to use as read-alouds to younger children.

Freeman, Judy. *Books Kids Will Sit Still For 3: A Read-Aloud Guide.* Westport, CT: Libraries Unlimited, 2006.

Not just limited to picture books, Freeman has created a guide to books to use as readalouds for a wide age range. She annotates her lists, and has clear subject headings so librarians and teachers can find great books to read to families, classrooms, and groups at the library.

Lima, Carolyn W., and John A. Lima. *A to Zoo: Subject Access to Children's Picture Books.* 7th ed. Westport, CT: Libraries Unlimited, 2005.

This is a handy tool to find a long list of picture books by subject. It lists picture books by topic, and in a large main library you are likely to have many of the books listed. You can use this great reference book at a small library; find your topic and use your catalog to pinpoint which books your library owns. There is also a supplement, published in 2008.

New York Public Library. http://kids.nypl.org/reading/ recommended2.cfm?ListID=61

A list of 100 picture books everyone should know— adults and children alike! This Web site has lots of other lists, including multicultural booklists for children and themed lists on several topics.

Straub, Susan, and K. J. Dell'Antonia. *Reading with Babies, Toddlers, and Twos: A Guide to Choosing, Reading, and Loving Books Together.* Naperville, IL: Sourcebooks, Inc., 2006.

Aimed at parents, this can also work for library staff members who serve babies, toddlers, and their parents. It is packed with lists of different books recommended for the youngest children, at various stages in their lives.

West Bloomfield Township Public Library. www.grow upreading. org/kickoff/index.php?section=550

This popular Michigan library site lists 100 books every child should have read to him or her before beginning kindergarten. The library followed this first list with "100 More Books to Read Before Kindergarten."

RECOMMENDED BOARD BOOKS

Ashman, Linda. *Babies on the Go.*

Baggott, Stella. <u>Babies Very First</u> series.

Blake, Michel. <u>Baby's Easy Open Board Books</u> series.

Boynton, Sandra. *Blue Hat, Green Hat.*

Boynton, Sandra. *Moo, Baa, La La La!*

Boynton, Sandra. *What's Wrong, Little Pookie?*

Cousins, Lucy. <u>Maisy</u> series.

Cummings, Pat. *My Aunt Came Back.*

Dale, Penny. *Ten in a Bed.*

Falconer, Ian. *Olivia's Opposites.*

Global Fund for Children. *Global Babies.*

Grover, Lorie Ann. *Hug Hug!*

Harper, Jamie. <u>Baby Bundt</u> series.

Hills, Tad. <u>Duck</u> series.

Henkes, Kevin. *Julius's Candy Corn.*

Henkes, Kevin. *Sheila Rae's Peppermint Stick.*

Hoban, Tana. *Black and White.*

Horacek, Petr. *Beep Beep.*

Horacek, Petr. *Choo Choo.*

Jocelyn, Marthe. <u>Ready For</u> series.

Katz, Karen. *Ten Tiny Tickles.*

Katz, Karen. *Where Is Baby's Belly Button?*

Kunhardt, Dorothy. *Pat the Bunny.*

Linenthal, Peter. *Look at Baby's House!*

McGuirk, Leslie. _Tucker_ series.

Miller, Margaret. *Baby Faces.*

Newgarden, Mark. _Bow Wow_ series.

Oxenbury, Helen. *All Fall Down.*

Oxenbury, Helen. *Clap Hands.*

Oxenbury, Helen. *Say Goodnight.*

Oxenbury, Helen. *Tickle, Tickle.*

Patricelli, Leslie. _Baby_ series.

Schindel, John. _Baby Animals_ series.

Stockham, Jess. _Just Like Us_ series.

Wells, Rosemary. _Max_ series.

Wilson, Karma. _Calico Cat_ series.

Yolen, Jane. *Time for Naps.*

RECOMMENDED PICTURE BOOKS

Amato, Mary. *The Chicken of the Family.*

Becker, Bonny. *A Visitor for Bear.*

Beaumont, Karen. *Move Over, Rover!*

Best, Cari. *Goose's Story.*

Best, Cari. *Shrinking Violet.*

Briant, Ed. *Don't Look Now.*

Broach, Elise. *When Dinosaurs Came with Everything.*

Brown, Margaret Wise. *Another Important Book.*

Bunting, Eve. *Our Library.*

Burningham, John. *Magic Bed.*

Busse, Sarah Martin. *Banjo Granny.*

Capucilli, Alyssa. *Katy Duck Is a Caterpillar.*

Carle, Eric. *Mister Seahorse.*

Chodos-Irvine, Margaret. *Best Best Friends.*

Collington, Peter. *Clever Cat.*

Crews, Nina. *Below.*

Cronin, Doreen. *Bounce.*

Cronin, Doreen. *Diary of a Worm.*

Cuyler, Margery. *Skeleton Hiccups.*

DePalma, Mary Newell. *A Grand Old Tree.*

DeTerlizzi, Tony. *Jimmy Zangwow's Out-of-this-World Moon Pie Adventure.*

Dewan, Ted. *Crispin and the 3 Little Pigs.*

Dillon, Leo, and Diane Dillon. *Mother Goose on the Loose.*

Falconer, Ian. <u>Olivia</u> series.

Faller, Regis. *The Adventures of Polo* and *Polo: The Runaway Book.*

Fleming, Candace. *This Is the Baby.*

Fleming, Denise. *Buster Goes to Cowboy Camp.*

Fox, Mem. *Ten Little Fingers and Ten Little Toes.*

Frazee, Marla. *A Couple of Boys Have the Best Week Ever.*

French, Jackie. *Diary of a Wombat.*

Graham, Bob. *How to Heal a Broken Wing.*

Graham, Bob. *Oscar's Half Birthday.*

Grant, Judyann Ackerman. *Chicken Said "Cluck!"*

Gravett, Emily. *Monkey and Me.*

Grey, Mini. *The Adventures of the Dish and the Spoon.*

Grey, Mini. *Traction Man Is Here!*

Grimes, Nikki. *Welcome Precious.*

Harris, Robie H. *Maybe a Bear Ate It!*

Hartman, Bob. *The Wolf Who Cried Boy.*

Hayes, Sarah. *Dog Day.*

Hendry, Diana. *The Very Noisy Night.*

Henkes, Kevin. *Kitten's First Full Moon.*

Henkes, Kevin. *Old Bear.*

Henkes, Kevin. *Wemberly Worried.*

Hicks, Barbara Jean. *Jitterbug Jam.*

Hindley, Judy. *Eyes, Nose, Fingers and Toes: First Book About You.*

Hines, Anna Grossnickle. *1, 2, Buckle My Shoe.*

Inkpen, Mick. *Roly and Kipper.*

Isadora, Rachel. *Peekaboo Morning.*

Knudsen, Michelle. *Library Lion.*

Kohara, Kazuno. *Ghosts in the House!*

Krosoczka, Jarrett J. *Punk Farm.*

Lindgren, Barbro. *Benny and the Binky.*

Meyers, Susan. *Everywhere Babies.*

Newman, Jeff. *Hippo! No, Rhino!*

Nye, Naomi Shihab. *Baby Radar.*

Perkins, Lynne Rae. *Snow Music.*

Portis, Antoinette. *Not a Box.*

Richards, Chuck. *Critter Sitter.*

Rohmann, Eric. *A Kitten Tale.*

Rosenthal, Amy Krouse. *Duck! Rabbit!*

Sandburg, Carl. *The Huckabuck Family and How They Raised Popcorn in Nebraska and Quit and Came Back.*

Seeger, Laura Vaccaro. <u>Dog and Bear</u> series.

Seeger, Laura Vaccaro. *First the Egg.*

Seeger, Laura Vaccaro. *One Boy.*

Shannon, David. *The Rain Came Down.*

Shulevitz, Uri. *So Sleepy Story.*

Shulman, Lisa. *Old MacDonald Had a Woodshop.*

Sierra, Judy. *Thelonius Monster's Sky High Pie.*

Sierra, Judy. *Wild About Books.*

Swanson, Susan. *A House in the Night.*

Sweet, Melissa. *Carmine: A Little More Red.*

Taback, Simms. *This Is the House That Jack Built.*

Thong, Roseanne. *Tummy Girl.*

Ward, Helen. *Hungry Hen.*

Watt, Melanie. *Scaredy Squirrel.*

Weeks, Sarah. *Two Eggs Please.*

Wells, Rosemary. *Ruby's Beauty Shop.*

Wheeler, Lisa. *Jazz Baby.*

Wiesner, David. *Flotsam.*

Willems, Mo. *Knuffle Bunny.*

PICTURE BOOKS ALL YOUNG CHILDREN SHOULD KNOW

Allard, Harry. *Miss Nelson Is Missing!*

Barton, Byron. *The Little Red Hen.*

Bemelmans, Ludwig. *Madeline.*

Bridwell, Norman. *Clifford the Big Red Dog.*

Brown, Margaret Wise. *Goodnight Moon.*

Brown, Margaret Wise. *The Runaway Bunny.*

Burton, Virginia Lee. *The Little House.*

Burton, Virginia Lee. *Mike Mulligan and His Steam Shovel.*

Carle, Eric. *The Very Hungry Caterpillar.*

Crews, Donald. *Freight Train.*

Daugherty, James. *Andy and the Lion.*

DePaola, Tomie. *Strega Nona.*

Emberley, Ed. *Go Away, Big Green Monster!*

Falconer, Ian. *Olivia.*

Feiffer, Jules. *Bark, George.*

Fleming, Denise. *Mama Cat Hat Three Kittens.*

Freeman, Don. *Corduroy.*

Gag, Wanda. *Millions of Cats.*

Galdone, Paul. *The Three Bears.*

Guarino, Deborah. *Is Your Mama a Llama?*

Henkes, Kevin. *Kitten's First Full Moon.*

Hill, Eric. *Where's Spot?*

Hoban, Russell. *Bread and Jam for Frances.*

Hughes, Shirley. *Alfie Gets in First.*

Hutchins, Pat. *Rosie's Walk.*

Johnson, Crockett. *Harold and the Purple Crayon.*

Kasza, Keiko. *The Wolf's Chicken Stew.*

Keats, Ezra Jack. *The Snowy Day.*

Keats, Ezra Jack. *Whistle for Willie.*

Krauss, Ruth. *The Carrot Seed.*

Leaf, Munro. *The Story of Ferdinand.*

Lionni, Leo. *Swimmy.*

London, Jonathan. *Froggy Gets Dressed.*

Marshall, James. *George and Martha.*

Martin, Bill, Jr. *Brown Bear, Brown Bear, What Do You See?*

Martin, Bill, Jr. *Chicka Chicka Boom Boom.*

McCloskey, Robert. *Make Way for Ducklings.*

Meddaugh, Susan. *Martha Speaks.*

Numeroff, Laura. *If You Give a Mouse a Cookie.*

Opie, Iona. *My Very First Mother Goose.*

Potter, Beatrix. *The Tale of Peter Rabbit.*

Rathmann, Peggy. *Good Night, Gorilla.*

Rey, H. A. *Curious George.*

Rohmann, Eric. *My Friend Rabbit.*

Scieszka, Jon. *The True Story of the 3 Little Pigs by A. Wolf.*

Sendak, Maurice. *Where the Wild Things Are.*

Seuss, Dr. *Horton Hatches the Egg.*

Seuss, Dr. *Horton Hears a Who!*

Shannon, David. *No, David!*

Shaw, Charles G. *It Looked Like Spilt Milk.*

Sis, Peter. *Fire Truck.*

Slobodkina, Esphyr. *Caps for Sale.*

Steig, William. *Doctor DeSoto.*

Steig, William. *Sylvester and the Magic Pebble.*

Van Allsburg, Chris. *The Polar Express.*

Viorst, Judith. *Alexander and the Terrible, Horrible, No Good, Very Bad Day.*

Waber, Bernard. *Ira Sleeps Over.*

Waber, Bernard. *Lyle, Lyle Crocodile.*

Willems, Mo. *Don't Let the Pigeon Drive the Bus.*

Willems, Mo. *Knuffle Bunny.*

Williams, Vera B. *A Chair for My Mother.*

Wood, Audrey. *The Napping House.*

Yolen, Jane. *How Do Dinosaurs Say Good Night?*

Zion, Gene. *Harry the Dirty Dog.*

PICTURE BOOKS OF TOPICAL INTEREST TO PARENTS

Adoption

Carlson, Nancy. *My Family Is Forever.*

Coste, Marion. *Finding Joy.*

Curtis, Jamie Lee. *Tell Me Again About the Night I Was Born.*

DePaola, Tomie. *A New Barker in the House.*

Friedrich, Molly. *You're Not My Real Mother!*

Kasza, Keiko. *A Mother for Choco.*

Krishnaswami, Uma. *Bringing Asha Home.*

Lears, Laurie. *Megan's Birthday Tree: A Story About Open Adoption.*

Lewis, Rose A. *Every Year on Your Birthday.*

Okimoto, Jean Davies. *The White Swan Express: A Story About Adoption.*

Parr, Todd. *We Belong Together: A Book About Adoption and Families.*

Rosenberg, Liz. *We Wanted You.*

Death

Burrowes, Adjoa. *Grandma's Purple Flowers.*

DePaola, Tomie. *Nana Upstairs and Nana Downstairs.*

Godfrey, Jan. *The Cherry Blossom Tree: A Grandfather Talks about Life and Death.*

Joslin, Mary. *The Goodbye Boat.*

Raschka, Chris. *The Purple Balloon.*

Rosen, Michael. *Michael Rosen's Sad Book.*

Divorce

Brown, Laurie Krasny. *Dinosaurs Divorce.*

Coffelt, Nancy. *Fred Stays with Me!*

Cole, Babette. *The Un-Wedding.*

Coy, John. *Two Old Potatoes and Me.*

Grindley, Sally. *A New Room for William.*

Masurel, Claire. *Two Homes.*

Spelman, Cornelia. *Mama and Daddy Bear's Divorce.*

Gay and Lesbian Families

Brannen, Sarah. *Uncle Bobby's Wedding.*

DePaola, Tomie. *Oliver Button Is a Sissy.*

Fierstein, Harvey. *The Sissy Duckling.*

Gonzalez, Rigoberto. *Antonio's Card.*

Parr, Todd. *The Family Book.*

Parr, Todd. *It's Okay to Be Different.*

Polacco, Patricia. *In Our Mothers' House.*

Richardson, Justin. *And Tango Makes Three.*

New Baby

Anholdt, Catherine. *Sophie and the New Baby.*

Ballard, Robin. *When I Am a Sister.*

Brown, Marc. *Arthur's Baby.*

Galbraith, Kathryn. *Waiting for Jennifer.*

Harris, Robie. *Hi New Baby!*

Henkes, Kevin. *Julius, the Baby of the World.*

Hoban, Russell. *A Baby Sister for Frances.*

Keats, Ezra Jack. *Peter's Chair.*

London, Jonathan. *Froggy's Baby Sister.*

Look, Lenore. *Henry's First-Moon Birthday.*

Mario, Heidi Stetson. *I'd Rather Have an Iguana.*

Schwartz, Amy. *A Teeny Tiny Baby.*

Walter, Mildred Pitts. *My Mama Needs Me.*

POPULAR TOPICS FOR PRESCHOOLERS

Alphabet

Abrams, Pam. *Now I Eat My ABC's.*

Anno, Mitsumasa. *Anno's Alphabet.*

Aylesworth, Jim. *Naughty Little Monkeys.*

Bruel, Nick. *Bad Kitty* and *Poor Puppy.*

Dugan, Joanne. *ABC NYC: A Book about Seeing New York City.*

Feelings, Muriel, and Tom Feelings. *Jambo Means Hello.*

Fleming, Denise. *Alphabet Under Construction.*

Gag, Wanda. *ABC Bunny.*

Jay, Alison. *A Child's First Alphabet Book.*

Lobel, Anita. *Animal Antics: A to Z.*

Martin, Bill, Jr. *Chicka Chicka Boom Boom.*

McLeod, Bob. *SuperHero ABC.*

Pearle, Ida. *A Child's Day: An Alphabet of Play.*

Shapiro, Zachary. *We're All in the Same Boat.*

Counting

Bang, Molly. *Ten, Nine, Eight.*

Berry, Lynne. *Duck Dunks.*

Cabrera, Jane. *Ten in a Bed.*

Crews, Donald. *Ten Black Dots.*

Feelings, Muriel, and Tom Feelings. *Moja Means One.*

Gorbachev, Valeri. *Christopher Counting.*

Hines, Anna Grossnickle. *1, 2, Buckle My Shoe.*

Jay, Alison. *1 2 3: A Child's First Counting Book.*

McLimans, David. *Gone Fishing: Ocean Life by the Numbers.*

Mockford, Caroline. *Cleo's Counting Book.*

Otoshi, Kathryn. *One.*

Yates, Philip. *Ten Little Mummies: An Egyptian Counting Book.*

Dinosaurs

Barton, Byron. *Dinosaurs, Dinosaurs.*

Broach, Elise. *When Dinosaurs Came with Everything.*

Carrick, Carol. *Patrick's Dinosaurs.*

Donnelly, Liza. *Dinosaur's Halloween.*

Foreman, Michael. *The Littlest Dinosaur.*

Grambling, Lois. *Can I Have a Stegosaurus, Mom? Can I Please?*

Hearn, Drake. *Dad's Dinosaur Day.*

Hennessey, B. G. *The Dinosaur Who Lived in My Backyard.*

Lund, Deb. *All Aboard the Dinotrain.*

Martin, Linda. *When Dinosaurs Go to School.*

McMullan, Kate. *I'm Bad!*

Plourde, Lynn. *Dino Pets.*

Pulver, Robin. *Mrs. Toggle and the Dinosaur.*

Shea, Bob. *Dinosaur vs. Bedtime.*

Stickland, Paul, and Henrietta Stickland. *Dinosaur Roar!*

Wild, Margaret. *My Dearest Dinosaur.*

Yolen, Jane. <u>How Do Dinosaurs Say Goodnight?</u> series.

Going to School

Anholt, Laurence. *Billy and the New Big School.*

Carlson, Nancy. *Look Out Kindergarten, Here I Come!*

Cazet, Denys. *Born in the Gravy.*

Child, Lauren. *I Am Too Absolutely Small for School.*

Cocca-Leffler, Maryann. *Mr. Tanen's Ties.*

Flood, Nancy. *I'll Go to School If . . .*

Hest, Amy. *Off to School, Baby Duck!*

London, Jonathan. *Froggy Goes to School.*

McNaughton, Colin. *Once Upon an Ordinary School Day.*

Munsch, Robert. *We Share Everything!*

Novak, Matt. *Jazzbo Goes to School.*

O'Neill, Alexis. *The Recess Queen.*

O'Neill, Alexis. *The Worst Best Friend.*

Poydar, Nancy. *First Day, Hooray!*

Rosenberry, Vera. *Vera's First Day of School.*

Schwartz, Amy. *Annabelle Swift, Kindergartner.*

Slate, Joseph. *Miss Bindergarten Gets Ready for Kindergarten.*

Wells, Rosemary. *Timothy Goes to School.*

Wright, Michael. *Jake Starts School.*

Pirates

Augarde, Steve. *Barnaby Shrew, Black Daw and the Mighty Wedgewood.*

Blaustein, Muriel. *Jim Chimp's Story.*

Bradman, Tony. *Dilly and the Pirates.*

Dubowski, Cathy E. *Pirate School.*

Dyke, John. *Pigwig and the Pirates.*

Fox, Mem. *Tough Boris.*

Funke, Cornelia. *Pirate Girl.*

Gilman, Phoebe. *Grandma and the Pirates.*

Goldsack, Gaby. *Captain Calamity's Big Mistake.*

Hawkins, Colin, and Jacqui Hawkins. *Pirates.*

Helquist, Brett. *Roger, the Jolly Pirate.*

Hutchins, Pat. *One-Eyed Jake.*

Isadora, Rachel. *The Pirates of Bedford Street.*

Keats, Ezra Jack. *Maggie and the Pirate.*

Long, Melinda. *How I Became a Pirate.*

McFarland, Lyn Rossiter. *Pirates's Parrot.*

McNaughton, Colin. *Jolly Rogers and the Pirates of Captain Abdul.*

McPhail, David. *Edward and the Pirates.*

Morgan, Allen. *Matthew and the Midnight Pirates.*

Peppe, Rodney. *The Kettleship Pirates.*

Sharratt, Nick. *Mrs. Pirate.*

Tucker, Kathy. *Do Pirates Take Baths?*

Princess Stories

Andersen, Hans Christian. *Princess and the Pea.*

Auch, Mary Jane. *Princess and the Pizza.*

Bateman, Teresa. *Princesses Have a Ball.*

Carlow, Emma. *Kitty Princess and the Newspaper Dress.*

Claesson, Stig. *Sophie the Circus Princess.*

Cole, Babette. *Princess Smartypants.*

Coyle, Carmela. *Do Princesses Wear Hiking Boots?*

Dale, Penny. *Princess, Princess.*

DeFelice, Cynthia. *The Real, True Dulcie Campbell.*

Dorrie, Doris. *Lottie's Princess Dress.*

Funke, Cornelia. *Princess Knight.*

Grambling, Lois. *Witch Who Wanted to Be a Princess.*

Grey, Mini. *The Very Smart Pea and the Princess-to-Be.*

Holabird, Katherine. *The Rose Fairy Princess.*

Horowitz, Dave. *Twenty-six Princesses.*

Kastner, Jill. *Princess Dinosaur.*

Kleven, Elisa. *The Paper Princess.*

Kleven, Elisa. *Paper Princess Finds Her Way.*

Lester, Helen. *Princess Penelope's Parrot.*

Levert, Mireille. *The Princess Who Had Almost Everything.*

Lum, Kate. *Princesses Are Not Quitters.*

Mack, Todd. *Princess Penelope.*

McCourt, Lisa. *Good night, Princess Pruney-Toes.*

Munsch, Robert. *Paper Bag Princess.*

Noyes, Deborah. *Red Butterfly.*

Oram, Hiawyn. *Princess Chamomile Gets Her Way.*

Perlman, Janet. *Penguin and the Pea.*

Priceman, Marjorie. *Princess Picky.*

Scrimger, Richard. *Princess Bun Bun.*

Tyler, Anne. *Tumble Tower.*

Wahl, Jan. *Cabbage Moon.*

Wood, Audrey. *The Princess and the Dragon.*

Trains

Awdry, W. <u>Thomas the Tank Engine</u> series.

Aylesworth, Jim. *Country Crossing.*

Crews, Donald. *Freight Train.*

Hubbell, Patricia. *Trains: Steaming! Pulling! Huffing!*

Lund, Deb. *All Aboard the Dinotrain.*

Merriam, Eve. *Train Leaves the Station.*

Neitzel, Shirley. *I'm Taking a Trip on My Train.*

Piper, Wally. *The Little Engine That Could.*

Rockwell, Anne. *Whoo! Whoo! Goes the Train.*

Sturges, Philemon. *I Love Trains!*

Voake, Charlotte. *Here Comes the Train.*

Vehicles

Barracca, Sal. *The Adventures of Taxi Dog.*

Barton, Byron. *My Car.*

Burton, Virginia Lee. *Katy and the Big Snow.*

Burton, Virginia Lee. *Mike Mulligan and His Steam Shovel.*

Coy, John. *Vroomaloom Zoom.*

Hurd, Thacher. *Zoom City.*

Maccarone, Grace. *Cars, Cars, Cars.*

McMullan, Kate. *I'm Dirty!* and *I Stink!*

Rockwell, Anne. *Things That Go.*

Steen, Sandra, and Susan Steen. *Car Wash.*

Zane, Alex. *Wheels on the Race Car.*

Zelinsky, Paul O. *Wheels on the Bus.*

Zimmerman, Andrea. *Trashy Town.*

Chapter 4

Readers' Advisory for Emergent Readers Ages Five to Six

Helping children who are learning how to read is a more involved process than helping older children and 'tweens looking for the latest fantasy series after they have devoured <u>Harry Potter</u> books. The emergent reader, who is usually age five or six, needs books that are both interesting and at his or her reading level. So doing readers' advisory with beginning readers can be a more involved process than doing it with other children.

First, you can steer the child and parent/caregiver to the beginning reader shelves. Books for this age level need to be "tried on," the way you try on shoes. While walking and talking, chat about what type of book the child may want. Does he or she like animal stories, or something funny? Once you get ideas of a few subjects that might appeal to that child, you can open up some of the books and see how much text and white space are on the page, what the vocabulary is like, and other factors that can help the child decide if this book is something he or she might be able to read.

Characteristics of Easy Reading Books

Easy readers have several specific characteristics that help determine whether they are right for a beginning reader. Is the text limited to short words that can be decoded, or sounded out, along with some simple sight words? Is the text limited to a few lines per page? Are most of the words just one or two syllables in length? Are the sentences fairly short? These factors can all help the beginning reader master that book.

Book design elements can also help greatly. Is there a lot of white space, so the eye can rest while figuring out a word? Do the illustrations help the reader guess at the text, by truly illustrating what is written? Is the typeface relatively large, with ample space between words? The best easy reading books all have these qualities.

Levels 1, 2, and 3

Many publishers are assigning levels to their easy readers, to help parents figure out if a particular book is right for their children. With the increase in reading in kindergarten, there are far more Level 1 books than there were just a few years ago. Level 1 books usually have just one line of text per page, and the illustrations are designed to help the child guess what the text is saying. Some Level 1 books even have rebus-style pictures set onto the line of text to make it easier to read. One of the finest very easy to read series is <u>Elephant and Piggie</u> by Mo Willems. These funny stories have brief cartoon dialogue balloons for text and repeat words so that the child can master these books quickly.

Level 2 books have a little more text; these are often the traditional easy readers we grew up with, like Helen Palmer's *Fish out of Water*. There may be four or six lines of text, but often first graders can read these by the midway point of the school year. Most easy readers fit in this category, from Arnold Lobel's <u>Frog and Toad</u> series to James Marshall's <u>Fox</u> books.

There are fewer Level 3 books; many of these have a whole page of text, but still have lots of white space and the same line spacing as Level 2 readers. The vocabulary is more demanding, with more syllables, but the books have great stories, and many students in the latter half of the first grade can read these. After mastering Level 3, most children are ready to move up to transitional fiction, which is covered in chapter 5. Look for the level on the front cover of the easy reader; not all have a level designation, but many do.

Helping Children Who Are Just Learning to Read

Figuring out a child's reading level can be difficult. Just asking what grade a young person is in helps a little, but it is not enough. Ask the child to name other books he or she has read recently; the child may be as tall as you are but will still be reading transitional fiction instead of longer novels. If the child is familiar with some easy readers, such as Dr. Seuss's *Green Eggs and Ham,* he or she may also be ready for many Level 2 readers. Following are some techniques for determining whether a book is appropriate for a child just learning how to read.

The Five-Finger Rule

One of the most difficult reading levels to determine is that of the child just learning how to read. You can use the "five-finger" rule for easy readers. Take the child aside (and away from other kids so the child won't be embarrassed) and have him or her read the first page to you. If the child needs help with a few words, that is fine; it means it is somewhat challenging. If he or she needs help with more than five words (hold up a finger every time you have to tell the child the word), then the book is too difficult and will likely turn the child off of reading. You can teach this trick to the child's parents or caregivers as well, so they can use the five-finger rule with other books.

In many school districts, children start learning how to read in kindergarten, not first grade. So there is a greater demand for very simple, very easy books to read. The five-finger rule can really come in handy with those kindergartners. Also, you might find it necessary to purchase more very simple readers if your local schools have adopted this reading policy, sometimes referred to as "kindergarten is the new first grade." Try to find more very easy to read books, with only a few words per page, to meet that demand.

Lexile Levels

The Lexile Level of a book is calculated based on the book's vocabulary and other factors. Measuring the Lexile Level suitable for an individual child can only be done by testing in a classroom; it cannot be done in a library as the five-finger rule can. But many children and parents come into the library knowing the Lexile Level they need, because the teacher has given them the number. The books are not labeled with the Lexile Level, but there is a Web site you can use to identify books by Lexile Level number: www.lexile.com.

I recently helped a first grader who knew he could read Lexile Level 30. I looked up that number on the Lexile Web site and found a list of books; Dr. Seuss's *Green Eggs and Ham* was on the list, as were several other familiar easy readers. Using the Lexile number and Web site made it easier for me to suggest books that first grader could read with ease. The Web site also has tools to help a parent figure out the child's reading level.

History of Easy Readers

Easy readers were first published in the 1930s, beginning with the Dick and Jane series of basal readers. These books, about the idyllic suburban life of a family, were boring, but seemed to help first graders learn to read. However, many children found them so boring that they were turned off from reading. Dr. Seuss was challenged to write a fun and interesting easy reader in the 1950s, and he came up with *The Cat in the Hat*. He followed with other cartoonlike easy readers, and the format took off. Harper & Row (now HarperCollins) started its I Can Read series with Minarik's Little Bear books in 1957; they still publish some of the best easy readers available.

Favorite Easy Reader Series

Many of the easy readers I read as a child are still on the shelves; Dr. Seuss's books are great examples of easy readers with continuing popularity. Peggy Parish's Amelia Bedelia series is also still popular. Many authors write a series of easy readers, with the same characters in each book but a new story. They are similar to episodic television shows, in which the recurring characters become involved in new (and often funny) situations each time. Easy reader series usually do not have to be read in chronological order. Some novels for 'tweens have to be read in the order in which they are written, like J. K. Rowling's Harry Potter books, but that is not usually true for easy reader series. At the end of this chapter is a list of popular easy reader series.

Nonfiction

Children who ask for nonfiction may appreciate books above their grade level, because they want to look at the photographs. If the subject is of special interest to the child, like dinosaurs, he or she can handle much of the vocabulary even though the child normally doesn't read on that level. Offer a wide variety of reading levels when showing nonfiction books to children; they will pick out things that interest them and that they can read. Many children (and adults) enjoy nonfiction for recreational reading, especially if it is a topic they are interested in. Remember, some emergent readers want nonfiction books so they can look at the photographs. A few publishers release nonfiction easy readers; DK Publishers is probably the most prominent. They put level numbers on the book covers to help parents and children decide whether that book is right for them. The books have beautiful color photos set on white backgrounds and large-type text that provides simple information on the subject.

Easy Readers: An Important Step

Many children and their parents, eager to start the child's journey as an independent reader, check out lots of easy reader books. Luckily, many of these are also popular as movies or television shows, from the works of Dr. Seuss, to *Clifford the Big Red Dog*, Bill Cosby's *Little Bill*, and Minarik's *Little Bear*, so the kids will grab books about these familiar characters. But they can be turned off if the books are so difficult they are frustrating, so finding that right fit can be an important step in the readers' advisory process with this age group. If we take extra time to help them find books they can master, easy readers will lead these children to a lifelong love of reading.

Helpful Sources about Books for Emergent Readers

Following are two Web sites and one reference book on easy readers.

Barstow, Barbara, Lelsie Molnar, and Judith Riggle. *Beyond Picture Books.* 3rd ed. Westport, CT: Libraries Unlimited, 2007.

More than 3,500 easy readers are reviewed in this handy guide, which has a detailed subject index. Lexile Levels are given, as well as lists such as "200 Outstanding First Readers," which you can use when doing readers' advisory.

Geisel Award. http://www.ala.org/ala/mgrps/divs/alsc/awardsgrants/bookmedia/geiselaward/geiselabout/index.cfm

First presented in 2006, this award, named for Dr. Seuss (whose real name was Theodore Geisel), honors the authors and illustrators of the best beginning readers. There are both easy to read picture books and easy readers on the list of Geisel winners and honor books.

Lexile Levels. www.lexile.com/EntrancePageHtml.aspx?1

This site provides a list of books for each Lexile Level. It also contains helpful information for parents who want to work with their children who are learning how to read.

RECOMMENDED BEGINNING READER BOOKS

Individual Beginning Readers

Benchley, Nathaniel. *Sam the Minuteman.*

Berenstain, Stan and Jan. *The Berenstain Bears and the Spooky Old Tree.*

Bernier-Grand, Carmen T. *Juan Bobo: Four Folktales from Puerto Rico.*

Coerr, Eleanor. *Chang's Paper Pony.*

Coerr, Eleanor. *The Josefina Story Quilt.*

Cole, Joanna. *Bony-Legs.*

Eastman, P. D. *Are You My Mother?*

Eastman, P. D. *The Best Nest.*

Eastman, P. D. *Go, Dog, Go!*

Hoban, Russell. *A Bargain for Frances.*

Hoff, Syd. *Danny and the Dinosaur.*

Johnson, Crockett. *A Picture for Harold's Room.*

LeSieg, Theo (pseudonym for Dr. Seuss). *Ten Apples on Top.*

Minarik, Else Holmelund. *Cat and Dog.*

Minarik, Else, Holmelund. *No Fighting, No Biting!*

Monjo, F. N. *The Drinking Gourd.*

Palmer, Helen. *A Fish out of Water.*

Pomerantz, Charlotte. *The Outside Dog.*

Popular Easy to Read Series Books

Arnold, Tedd. <u>Fly Guy</u> series.

Byars, Betsy. <u>Golly Sisters</u> series.

Cazet, Denys. <u>Minnie and Moo</u> series.

Cosby, Bill. <u>Little Bill</u> series.

Guest, Elissa Haden. <u>Iris and Walter</u> series.

Lobel, Arnold. <u>Frog and Toad</u> series.

Marshall, James. <u>Fox</u> series.

Mills, Claudia. <u>Gus and Grandpa</u> series.

Minarik, Else Holmelund. <u>Little Bear</u> series.

O'Connor, Jane. <u>Fancy Nancy</u> *series.*

Parish, Peggy. <u>Amelia Bedelia</u> series.

Rylant, Cynthia. <u>Henry and Mudge</u> series.

Rylant, Cynthia. <u>High-Rise Private Eyes</u> series.

Rylant, Cynthia. <u>Mr. Putter and Tabby</u> series.

Rylant, Cynthia. <u>Poppleton</u> series.

Seuss, Dr. *The Cat and the Hat* (and several other books).

Sharmat, Marjorie Weinman. <u>Nate the Great</u> series.

Van Leeuwen, Jean. <u>Oliver and Amanda</u> series.

Willems, Mo. <u>Elephant and Piggie</u> series.

Wiseman, Bernard. <u>Morris and Boris</u> series.

Chapter 5

Readers' Advisory for Transitional Readers Ages Six to Eight

Once a five- or six-year-old has mastered beginning reader books, he or she can begin to read chapter books. Around age seven, many children can move up to easy chapter books, often referred to as transitional fiction. This chapter examines what transitional fiction is and how it bridges the gap between easy readers and novels for 'tweens.

What Is Transitional Fiction?

Transitional fiction can be suggested to children old enough to read chapter books. They have mastered easy readers; now those second and third graders are ready for longer books with chapters, but not quite ready for full-fledged juvenile novels like <u>Harry Potter</u> or even the <u>Little House on the Prairie</u> series. Most transitional books have chapters, interspersed with ink drawings to break up the text. The books have more white space and larger typefaces than longer juvenile novels, to help the child make the transition. Sometimes these are called bridge books or moving up fiction, because they are the easy chapter books that help a child move from easy readers to juvenile novels.

Easy Transitional Books

One of the more difficult situations you may face as a readers' advisor is trying to find independent reading books for a child who is moving up from easy readers, but for whom most transitional books are still too difficult. A perfect example of an easy moving up series is James Howe's Pinky and Rex. This series features chapters, a little more complex and a little longer than an easy reader, but still with lots of white space and color illustrations. Another series for this same age group is Kate DiCamillo's Mercy Watson, about a pet pig. The Mercy books have more text than an easy reader, laid out in paragraph form like a fiction book, but with more white space and with color illustrations. There are so few books for the "starting second grade" reader that kids will stay with easy readers longer than necessary because it is comfortable, or read picture books like Marc Brown's Arthur series because chapter books are just too daunting. Hopefully the publishing industry will issue more easy transitional books.

Popular Transitional Books

Once kids have mastered the easy transitional books, there are several great books and series to choose from. A recent "star" of the transitional category is Dav Pilkey's Captain Underpants books, because they contain a lot of illustrations to make the chapter format seem less challenging, and of course because of their outrageous humor and sense of fun. Many other moving up titles cannot be tackled until the end of second grade (because so many children read below grade level), but children soon catch up to series like Junie B. Jones, The Magic Tree House, Judy Moody, Time Warp Trio, The Bailey School Kids, and many more, which are often published only in paperback. David Adler's girl detective, Cam Jansen, has been popular for more than twenty years, and there are many others. Genre fiction really starts to emerge in transitional books, with an emphasis on humorous school stories, mystery stories, and sports (e.g., the books of Matt Christopher), but not so much fantasy, science fiction, or historical fiction. Of course, many second graders can tackle all of these categories because they read higher than their grade level, but many second graders and even third graders find the leap to novels difficult, so mastering transitional fiction is a key step in their literacy process.

Characteristics of Transitional Books

In 2008 I heard a great presentation at an American Library Association conference on transitional books, given by Andrea Zevenbergen and Allison Angell, in which they outlined some of the key aspects of and reasons children need transitional literature. Following are those characteristics:

- Short chapters, averaging six to eight pages each, with books averaging 60 to 100 pages total

- Reader-friendly font size and lots of white space

- A few illustrations per chapter

- Language and vocabulary accessible to second to fourth graders

- Issues relevant to this age group

- Episodic chapters

- Characters with unique but unchanging personalities

- Linear plot development

How Transitional Books Motivate Literacy

Andrea Zevenbergen and Allison Angell also discussed how transitional books facilitate and motivate a child's literacy skills development:

- They have some illustrations, large margins, large font, and short sentences.

- Contextual clues are often given.

- They help develop sustained attention on reading.

- They help develop decoding and reading fluency.

- The reader is motivated by perceptions of likely success.

- Somewhat challenging texts are optimal in enhancing motivation.

- There is interesting character development and suspense.

- The language is rhythmic and vivid, or there is humor that appeals to this age group.

Transitional books also facilitate a child's social and emotional development in the following ways:

- ◆ These books reflect common challenges.

- ◆ They enhance the child's feeling of industry and mastery.

- ◆ They expose the reader to social issues.

- ◆ They promote insight into others' way of thinking or living.

- ◆ Mastering transitional books gives the child a sense of self-esteem.

Where Are Transitional Books Shelved?

Zevenbergen and Angell's study included a survey of how libraries shelve and label transitional books. Only 31 percent shelved transitional books separately. This was a bit of a shock to me, because my library has always shelved them separately. The survey indicated that among those who do not shelve transitional books separately, 44 percent shelve them with the regular juvenile fiction (novels), 15 percent shelve them with easy readers, 13 percent shelve them depending on difficulty (dividing them between easy readers and juvenile novels), and 6 percent put them with series books. Also, 40 percent have some type of label or sticker indicating that a book is transitional. This presents a major problem: Where does a child go when he or she is ready to move from an easy reader to a transitional book? How can the child find them if they are not shelved separately? In your library, check to see where these books are shelved and determine whether this is serving your audience well.

On the positive side, more and more transitional books are being published (perhaps due to the popularity of <u>Captain Underpants</u>), and these are very popular. New series include Judy Moody's little brother, <u>Stink</u>, by Megan McDonald; the <u>Ivy and Bean</u> books by Annie Barrows; and <u>Alvin Ho</u> by Lenore Look. At the end of this chapter is a list of the transitional series that are currently popular.

Transitional Fiction: A Key Step in Reading

Transitional fiction is the bridge between easy readers and lengthy juvenile novels. If a child cannot master transitional fiction, he or she will often stop reading or become a reluctant reader, who never acquires enough skill to read for pleasure. There is currently a great deal of concern about boys not reading; it is often at ages seven and eight that they stop reading for fun and will only read for school-related reasons. So if we can help children find and enjoy transitional fiction, books that fit their reading abilities and interests, we have a better chance of them becoming lifelong readers. Discover which transitional books are in your library so you can offer them during readers' advisory.

Helpful Books and Web Sites on Transitional Fiction

Many children looking for transitional fiction look for series books, often on the paperback shelves. Following are some helpful tools, one reference book and a few Web sites, that you can use if a child wants to read a series in order. Not all of the series listed on these sites are transitional; series for 'tweens are also listed. But it is at the transitional stage that readers really take to reading series fiction, and in order, so you should find these sites helpful.

Books in a Series. www.monroe.lib.in.us/childrens/series list.html

Maintained by the Monroe Public Library in Indiana, this site lists thousands of children's book series. You can search by a series or by the author, and see in what order the books were published.

Juvenile Series and Sequels. www.mcpl.lib.mo.us/readers/series/juv/

The Mid-Continent Public Library in Missouri has a great site on children's book series, which can be searched by series name, author, series subject, or individual book title. It lists the books in order for those who prefer reading a series in published order. These are not just transitional series; use this for 'tweens and teens, too.

Thomas, Rebecca L., and Catherine Barr. *Popular Series Fiction for K–6 Readers: A Reading and Selection Guide.* Westport, CT: Libraries Unlimited, 2005.

An easy-to-use book listing popular children's series books in order; very often children want to read the series in the order the books are published.

Zevenbergen and Angell's Report. http://ala2008.wetpaint. com/page/Beyond+Frog+and+Toad:+Transitional+ Books+for+Children

At this site you will find the handout for the ALA Conference presentation "Beyond Frog and Toad," presented by Andrea Zevenbergen and Allison Angell, discussed in this chapter.

EASY TRANSITIONAL BOOKS

Brisson, Pat. *Bertie's Picture Day*.

Brisson, Pat. *Hot Fudge Hero*.

Catalanotto, Peter, and Pamela Schembri. <u>2nd Grade Friends</u> series.

Christopher, Matt. *The Dog That Stole Football Plays*.

Christopher, Matt. *The Dog That Stole Home*.

DiCamillo, Kate. <u>Mercy Watson</u> series.

Edwards, Michelle. *Pa Lia's First Day*.

Elliott, David. <u>Cool Crazy Crickets</u> series.

Howe, Jame. <u>Pinky and Rex</u> series.

Stevenson, James. <u>Mud Flat</u> series.

Yolen, Jane. <u>Commander Toad</u> series.

POPULAR TRANSITIONAL SERIES

Abbott, Tony. <u>The Secrets of Droon</u> series.

Adler, David. <u>Cam Jansen</u> series.

Averill, Esther. <u>Jenny the Cat</u> series.

Barrows, Annie. <u>Ivy and Bean</u> series.

Cameron, Ann. *The Stories Julian Tells* (and sequels).

Dadey, Debbie, et al. <u>Bailey School Kids</u> series.

Danziger, Paula. <u>Amber Brown</u> series.

DePaola, Tomie. <u>26 Fairmount Avenue</u> series.

Duffy, Betsy. <u>Cody</u> series.

Gannett, Ruth S. <u>My Father's Dragon</u> series.

Greenburg, Dan. <u>Zack Files</u> series.

Greenburg, J. C. <u>Andrew Lost</u> series.

Greene, Stephanie. <u>Owen Foote</u> series.

Greenwald, Sheila. <u>Rosy Cole</u> series.

Grimes, Nikki. *Make Way for Dyamonde Daniels* (and sequels).

Holm, Jennifer. <u>Babymouse</u> graphic novel series.

Hurwitz, Johanna. <u>Park Pals</u> series.

Hurwitz, Johanna. <u>Russell and Elisa</u> series.

Jacobson, Jennifer. <u>Andy Shane</u> series.

Kerrin, Jessica Scott. <u>Martin Bridge</u> series.

Landon, Lucinda. <u>Meg Mackintosh</u> series.

Le Guin, Ursula. <u>Catwings</u> series.

Lewis, Maggie. <u>Morgy</u> series.

Lin, Grace. <u>The Year of the Dog</u> series.

Look, Lenore. <u>Alvin Ho</u> series.

Look, Lenore. <u>Ruby Lu</u> series.

Lowry, Lois. <u>Goonie Bird</u> series.

Marshall, James. <u>Rats on the Roof</u> series.

McDonald, Megan. <u>Judy Moody</u> series.

From *Readers' Advisory for Children and 'Tweens* by Penny Peck.
Santa Barbara, CA: Libraries Unlimited. Copyright © 2010.

McDonald, Megan. Stink series.

McMullan, Kate. Dragon Slayer's Academy series.

Osborne, Mary Pope. Magic Tree House series.

Park, Barbara. Junie B. Jones series.

Pennypacker, Sara. Clementine series.

Pilkey, Dav. Captain Underpants series.

Pilkey, Dav. Ricky Ricotta series.

Proimos, James. Johnny Mutton series.

Quackenbush, Robert. Miss Mallard Mystery series.

Riddell, Chris. Ottoline series.

Roy, Ron. A to Z Mysteries series.

Scieszka, Jon. Time Warp Trio series.

Smith, Alexander McCall. Akimbo series.

Stilton, Geronimo. Geronimo Stilton series.

Trine, Greg. Melvin Beederman Superhero series.

VanDraanen, Wendelin. Shredderman series.

Whybrow, Ian. Little Wolf series.

Wojciechowski, Susan. Beany series.

Wong, Janet S. Minn and Jake series.

POPULAR SINGLE TRANSITIONAL TITLES

Blume, Judy. *Freckle Juice.*

Burgess, Melvin. *The Copper Treasure.*

Brown, Jeff. *Flat Stanley.*

Cleary, Beverly. *Muggie Maggie.*

Coerr, Eleanor. *Sadako and the Thousand Paper Cranes.*

Cohen, Barbara. *Molly's Pilgrim.*

Cowley, Joy. *Chicken Feathers.*

Dahl, Roald. *Fantastic Mr. Fox.*

Dahl, Roald. *The Magic Finger.*

Dalgliesh, Alice. *The Courage of Sarah Noble.*

DuBois, William Pene. *Lazy Tommy Pumpkinhead.*

Haddix, Margaret Peterson. *The Girl with 500 Middle Names.*

Haddix, Margaret Peterson. *Say What?*

Hesse, Karen. *Sable.*

Hest, Amy. *Remembering Mrs. Rossi.*

Jacobson, Jennifer. *Winnie Dancing on Her Own.*

Johnson, Angela. *Maniac Monkeys on Magnolia Street.*

King-Smith, Dick. *Lady Lollipop.*

MacLachlan, Patricia. *Sarah, Plain and Tall.*

Perkins, Mitali. *Rickshaw Girl.*

Porte, Barbara. *Ruthann and Her Pig.*

Rodowsky, Colby. *Not My Dog.*

Smith, Doris Buchanan. *A Taste of Blackberries.*

Soto, Gary. *The Skirt.*

Taylor, Mildred D. *The Friendship.*

Taylor, Mildred D. *The Gold Cadillac.*

Taylor, Mildred D. *The Well.*

Walter, Mildred Pitts. *Justin and the Best Biscuits in the World.*

Williams, Vera B. *Amber Was Brave, Essie Was Smart.*

Chapter 6

Readers' Advisory for 'Tweens

'Tween is the current term for children who are pre-teen—old enough to be without a babysitter at home, but too young to be unsupervised at many places outside the home. Often, a 'tween comes to a library without a parent or caregiver, on the way home from school. 'Tweens are ages nine to twelve, which means they are usually in fourth through seventh grades. They are an influential group in the marketplace, with quite a bit of disposable income. For example, in 2007 *Business Week* reported that there were over 21 million 'tweens in the United States, with more than $50 billion in disposable income! Many of the movies, television shows, and music recordings that appeal to 'tweens are in the "top ten." This includes books as well; 'tweens greatly influence which novels for youth are popular, which sell the most, and which books become films. They often are adept readers who enjoy a variety of books and can read at or above their grade levels. Others fall into the group of 'tweens who are classified as "reluctant readers" and read below grade level. They may have a learning disability like dyslexia, but librarians can still find books they might enjoy.

Genre Fiction for 'Tweens

Just like fiction for adults, novels for children and 'tweens often fall into specific categories. Unlike some adults, children read across genres quite readily. Some of the first children's books were fantasy: Baum's *The Wizard of Oz*, Carroll's *Alice in Wonderland*, and so forth. Historical fiction was also popular at one time, such as Howard Pyle's books based on Arthurian legends. Once you conduct the readers' advisory interview (discussed in chapter 1) with a 'tween, you might discover the 'tween likes certain types of books, like humor or animal stories. Many genres are available in children's fiction; following is a review of the popular authors and distinctive qualities of those genres.

Fantasy

Fantasy has many of the imaginary creatures seen in folk and fairy tales—unicorns, dragons, wizards, and other magical elements. J. R. R. Tolkien's books; C. S. Lewis's <u>Narnia</u> series; and the wonderful books by Lloyd Alexander, Ursula Le Guin, and Susan Cooper all have folktale elements of witches, little people, dragons, etc. Then there are books featuring characters who have magical powers, like Rowling's <u>Harry Potter</u> books, Mary Norton's <u>The Borrowers</u> series, Lucy Boston's <u>Green Knowe</u> books, and many others. These add traditional magical beings to original plots. Because of the success of <u>Harry Potter</u>, more fantasy series are being published than ever before. When a series catches on, it can be so popular that you may not be able to keep copies on the shelf. Rick Riordan's <u>Percy Jackson</u> books are very popular with both boys and girls.

Another popular feature of fantasy is animals that talk. Kenneth Grahame's *Wind in the Willows* is a great example, as are Milne's <u>Winnie the Pooh</u> books, E. B. White's *Charlotte's Web* or *Stuart Little*, George Selden's *The Cricket in Times Square,* and Avi's <u>Poppy</u> series.

Humorous fantasy adds magic to the real world to make fun of the stuffy, over-serious world of adults. Lindgren's <u>Pippi Longstocking</u> and Travers' <u>Mary Poppins</u> are examples. <u>Harry Potter</u> also falls into this category. Roald Dahl's *Matilda* is a great example of fantasy mixed with humor.

Science Fiction

Related to fantasy, science fiction was not readily found in children's books until relatively recently. A hundred years ago, children read Jules Verne, but he didn't write specifically for young readers. Kids also read science fiction comic books. But Madeleine L'Engle's *A Wrinkle in Time* really opened the door to science fiction for 'tweens. Her work is still popular, and has inspired other authors such as William Sleator, John Christopher, and Sylvia Waugh. Many adult science fiction authors also wrote books just for kids, most notably Andre Norton, Isaac Asimov, and Robert Heinlein. Margaret Peterson Haddix writes very popular stories set in the near future, including the <u>Among the Hidden</u> series. Science fiction is very popular in movies and television, so it is understandable that more children's novels deal with space travel, the future, aliens, and other elements of this genre.

Contemporary Realistic Fiction

One of the largest and most popular genres, contemporary realistic fiction for children includes family stories, school stories, problem stories, and just about anything else that doesn't fall into one of the other genres. This genre includes more multicultural characters and themes and can address current issues like racism, terrorism, poverty, or homelessness. These books can also open children's minds to gender issues, nontraditional families, and other political themes. The best realistic fiction has strong, believable characters, important themes, truthful depictions, and an authentic voice, without pandering to children or underestimating their intelligence.

Published in the 1940s and 1950s, Eleanor Estes's books were often set in the city, almost a children's version of novels, like Betty Smith's *A Tree Grows in Brooklyn*. Estes's *Hundred Dresses* is a poignant look at prejudice. Beverly Cleary's humorous chapter books also address social issues in a subtle way; for example, in *Ramona and Her Father*, Dad is unemployed. Louise Fitzhugh's *Harriet the Spy* deals with gender identity; Judy Blume's books often address issues like puberty; and E. L. Konigsburg's, S. E.Hinton's, and Jerry Spinelli's books often discuss "fitting in." Many of these books address realistic, controversial issues, but temper them with humor and thoughtfulness. Even books about death, like Lois Lowry's *A Summer to Die* or Marion Dane Bauer's *On My Honor*, offer hope. Many of the novels by Jacqueline Woodson feature African American characters in a contemporary and realistic, not historical, setting.

Humor

An offshoot of realistic fiction is humorous fiction (there are also humorous fantasy novels, mysteries, etc.). Humor for children can be refreshing, but of course, "Dying is easy, comedy is hard," as a great actor once said. Great humor is difficult to achieve, but when it is done well, it can be very popular with all children, especially as a classroom or family read-aloud. Examples of realistic humor include Betsy Byars's <u>Bingo Brown</u> books, Lois Lowry's books about Anastasia Krupnik and her brother Sam, and Barbara Robinson's books about the horrible Herdmans.

Jeff Kinney's <u>Diary of a Wimpy Kid</u> series is very popular. Fantasy humor includes Mary Rodger's *Freaky Friday*. Bruce Hale's <u>Chet Gecko</u> mysteries are funny spoofs of old movies. Humorous historical fiction includes many books by Sid Fleischman, such as the gold rush era adventure *By the Great Horn Spoon!* (three genres in one—humor, adventure, and historical fiction!). John Fitzgerald's very funny <u>Great Brain</u> series is set in the late 1890s in Utah.

Mystery/Horror/Gothic

When asked which books they read as children, many children's authors and librarians answer <u>Nancy Drew and the Hardy Boys</u>. These mystery series were thought to be "chewing gum for the mind," but were popular when they first came out and are still popular now. In fact, mystery series in general are still in great demand, with characters that range from Cam Jansen to Encyclopedia Brown to Sammy Keyes. Newbery Medalist Laurence Yep has created a series set in San Francisco's Chinatown, featuring a Chinese American girl detective, sort of a Chinese American Nancy Drew. Betsy Byars created Herculeah Jones. Children's mystery stories are often set in the here and now, but some are also historical fiction, like Philip Pullman's *Ruby in the Smoke,* set in Victorian England.

Because of the suspense, mysteries may appeal to children who say they don't like "reading." The best mysteries have probable plots, clues to help the reader solve the mystery, foreshadowing that is not too obvious, and great pacing and suspense. Many children also like the "scary" element of some mysteries. One of the most popular mystery series is the one about the Baudelaire orphans, by Lemony Snicket. Another popular mystery is *Chasing Vermeer* by Blue Balliett, and its sequels, *The Wright 3* and *The Calder Game.* The <u>Sammy Keyes</u> mysteries by Wendelin VanDraanan have won several awards. Mysteries can be great to offer the 'tween who doesn't know what he or she wants to read.

Sports

Too often, sports novels offer formulaic plots with too much on-field or on-court action, so character development suffers. But the best sports novels for kids, like Bruce Brooks's *The Moves Make the Man,* offer believable characters, exciting action, and realistic plots. The best-known sports author is probably the late Matt Christopher; his books are formulaic but popular with young readers. John Tunis was an early proponent of the sports novel for youth, and Scott Corbett, Dean Hughes, and Alfred Slote also write for this genre. R. R. Knudson was one of the few women writers of the sports novel, and her books offer female protagonists and very realistic sports action. John Feinstein has written a series of mystery sports novels featuring a boy and girl as the main characters, which gives them a wide appeal.

Animal Stories

There are two kinds of animal stories. Talking animal stories, like *Charlotte's Web*, are fantasy. The realistic animal story is equally popular, with books like *Old Yeller*, Naylor's Shiloh series, *Where the Red Fern Grows* by Wilson Rawls, and books by Jean Craighead George or Walt Morey. In these books, the animals are realistically portrayed, but offer the reader a chance to involve their emotions. Most of these novels focus on dogs or horses, and to a lesser degree on cats or other animals. The best of them don't manipulate the reader's emotions, but offer universal truths and realistic characters. These realistic animal stories also appeal to 'tweens seeking adventure novels.

Adventure

Many adventure stories are also historical fiction, from Stevenson's *Treasure Island* to the books by Leon Garfield and Iain Lawrence. Some adventure books originally written for adults, like Jack London's *Call of the Wild* and *White Fang*, are very popular with middle schoolers. They are action-packed stories, often set in unusual locales, such as at sea—and they feature pirates, explorers, journeys and quests, and villains. Some adventure books are set in the present and feature a boy or girl who has to survive in the wilderness; Gary Paulsen's *Hatchet* is a great example. The adventure story can have heightened realism, and fewer ambiguous heroes and villains than realistic fiction, but both historical and modern adventure should at least be plausible, if not probable. Adventure novels are great to recommend to a 'tween whose favorite TV show is *Survivor*.

Historical Fiction

Historical fiction is one of the oldest and most popular genres in children's fiction; it is certainly my personal favorite. From the autobiographical novels of Laura Ingalls Wilder, to the many books by Scott O'Dell, to the recent work by Karen Cushman, this genre offers books that adults as well as 'tweens can read and admire. Some books we think of as historical fiction were actually realistic fiction at the time they were written; Alcott's *Little Women* comes to mind. Historical fiction can be very dramatic, with great characters, but must be historically accurate to be truly notable. Children may not be able to catch the errors, but adults will, and the accurate historical novel can add to a child's understanding of history (whereas an inaccurate historical novel can lead to misunderstanding and confusion), but it shouldn't require the reader to have a great deal of knowledge of the time period to be able to understand the novel.

Historical fiction offers many exciting, dramatic plots, and often presents a clear sense of right and wrong. Look for stories in which the characters speak in a realistic way for that time period and do not sound like contemporary kids. Cornelia Meigs and Rachel Fields were two children's book authors in the early twentieth century who wrote historical fiction. They were followed by Marguerite de Angeli (*Door in the Wall*) and Elizabeth Coatsworth. Others whose works are still read include Elizabeth George Speare (*Witch of Blackbird Pond*), Rosemary Sutcliff, and Esther Forbes (*Johnny Tremain*).

The Scott O'Dell Award is given to a historical fiction book for children; it is named after the author of *Island of the Blue Dolphins*. Many Newbery Medal and Honor books are historical fiction for grades five through eight. This appears to be a very popular genre.

Of course, school librarians and teachers appreciate the added value that historical fiction can bring to the classroom; it can offer great literature and a love of reading while conveying information that also relates to the history and social studies curriculum. If a child is asking for a book to use for a book report, historical fiction can often fill the bill.

It seems as though most historical fiction for children is set in Europe or in the United States, but there is also historical fiction that represents the non-Western world. A few years ago the Newbery Medal went to *A Single Shard*, by Linda Sue Park, which is set in medieval Korea.

Genre Labels Can Help

Of course, each library has its own genre designations; mine are based on the children's literature classes I took and on books such as Zena Sutherland's *Children and Books.* Through an effective readers' advisory interview, you can often discern what genres a specific 'tween enjoys. Many libraries put stickers indicating the genres on the spines of their juvenile fiction books. These can help staff and patrons find books they might like. A 'tween can tell if a book is a mystery, humorous, an adventure tale, and so forth. You don't need to separate the genres unless your collection is very large and unwieldy; just having the labels will be a great help. Many children's authors write in more than one genre, so having the labels can help readers find their favorite categories while still shelving the juvenile novels in order by author.

Book Awards

Award-winning books can also be effective offerings when doing readers' advisory. No book award has more influence on sales than the Newbery Medal, because Newbery winners don't go out of print, and are almost always found on the shelf of even the smallest branch library. Just what are these awards, and who chooses the recipients?

Newbery Medal

The Newbery Award is given to the author of the "most distinguished contribution to American literature for children." It goes to a book for the text, not the illustrations, and not for popularity or anything else. The award does have to go to an American, which is why Roald Dahl never won, and why J. K. Rowling's Harry Potter is not eligible. It is administered by the Association of Library Service to Children (ALSC), a division of the American Library Association (ALA). The Newbery Award was instituted in 1922; in 1937, the Caldecott Award was founded to award an illustrator for a similarly excellent work. There have also always been "honor" books, which receive a silver medal, compared to the winner's gold medal. For the past thirty years the Honor books have been limited to five per year (the committee doesn't have to name five, it just can't name more than five). A few years ago *Crispin: Cross of Lead* by Avi won the gold medal, and five honor books were named. All six titles are fiction aimed at middle schoolers, although nonfiction and books for younger readers are also eligible. But it is curious that most winners and honor books seem to fit the "middle school fiction (grades 6–8) category," which is perfect for 'tweens.

The 2005 winner, *Kira-Kira* by Cynthia Kadohata, is a middle school level historical fiction book, set in the 1950s. The 2006 winner, Lynne Rae Perkins's *Criss Cross*, is also a middle school novel. The 2009 winner is Neil Gaiman's *The Graveyard Book*, which is for ages twelve to fourteen.

The 2007 winner was *The Higher Power of Lucky* by Susan Patron, a former children's librarian in Los Angeles. It is a serious book, but for a wider age range than winners in the past few years: Lucky is a ten-year-old girl, and the book is aimed at grades four to six. But the three Newbery honor books from that year are all aimed at middle schoolers: *Penny from Heaven* by Jennifer L. Holm, *Hattie Big Sky* by Kirby Larson, and *Rules* by Cynthia Lord. So if you are looking for 'tween "quality" novels, a common request from parents, try the Newbery Medal and honor books. See below for the Web site listing these.

Caldecott Medal

The Caldecott Medal is awarded for artwork, so if the text is a little "ordinary," that doesn't matter. If the text is downright bad, or inaccurate, the committee can take that into consideration, because the award considers "the excellence of pictorial interpretation of the story"; that is, if the story is really bad, it won't matter if the pictures are beautiful. Most of the Caldecott winners and runners-up are books for readers younger than the 'tween audience. They are great for those in preschool through first grade (discussed in chapter 3). But there is one special exception—the Caldecott winner for 2008 was Brian Selznick's *The Invention of Hugo Cabret*, an illustrated novel that is perfect for the 'tween reader.

Other Awards

There are more than 100 children's book awards; nearly every state has one. Check the Internet to see if your state has a children's book award; you will want to stock the winners and nominees, especially if schoolchildren get to vote.

The Jane Addams Award is given to the book that best promotes peace. The Batchelder Award is given to a book translated into English and published in the United States that was originally published in a foreign language. On the international playing field, the Hans Christian Andersen Award goes to an author or illustrator for lifetime achievement.

Two genre awards can help you find books for 'tweens looking for that genre. The Edgar Award, for mysteries, has categories for both young adult and juvenile. Named after Edgar Allan Poe, the award is given by the Mystery Writers of America (www.theedgars.com). Past winners include Blue Balliett, Wendelin Van Draanen, Joan Lowery Nixon, and Tony Abbott.

In the genre of historical fiction there is the Scott O'Dell Award, discussed previously in this chapter. The Web site for this award is www.scottodell.com/odellaward.html. The award is given to one book each year that is either a juvenile or young adult novel. Past winners include Laurie Halse Anderson, Christopher Paul Curtis, Ellen Klages, Karen Hesse, and Louise Erdrich.

But nothing packs the punch of the Newbery. When a 'tween asks for a book for a book report, these winners are great to suggest, but also offer them when 'tweens want a recreational reading book.

Young Adult Books for 'Tweens

In many libraries, there are books in the young adult section that appeal to middle schoolers and some that only appeal to high schoolers, so the category has an informal division. Many children's areas in the library contain books for readers up to eighth grade, so middle schoolers use both the children's and young adult areas of the library with ease. When you are doing readers' advisory with tweens, remember that young adult books might appeal to them. Books such as S. E. Hinton's *The Outsiders* and Jerry Spinelli's *Star Girl* and *Smiles to Go*, as well as series like <u>Warriors</u> by Erin Hunter, the <u>Alice</u> books by Phyllis Reynolds Naylor, the <u>Princess Diaries</u> books by Meg Cabot, and the adventure books by Anthony Horowitz, are usually appropriate for older 'tweens.

S. E. Hinton's *The Outsiders* was one of the first books aimed directly at 'tweens (and written by a teen). Written when Hinton was sixteen and published in 1967, this book appeals to both 'tween boys and girls—to girls for the romance, to boys for the gangs. It is still popular with 'tweens, especially eleven- and twelve-year-olds, and was made into a successful movie that follows the book relatively closely. It was at about this same time (in the late 1960s) that libraries started to acknowledge that teens needed their own section, or at least a special shelving area, in the public library. Although the American Library Association started the young adult division in 1958 (YALSA), it really wasn't until the late 1960s and early 1970s that most public libraries started to have young adult areas.

Many young adult books are read by middle schoolers, which is part of the 'tween audience. Cormier's *The Chocolate War* is often assigned in eighth grade, and it is often the book that receives the most "censorship" complaints from parents. Judy Blume's *Forever*, written in 1975, has a depiction of teen sex that seventh and eighth graders read, but parents object to it. So when doing readers' advisory with 'tweens who want young adult books, you need to know what is in any book you offer, because some, like Blume's *Forever*, are probably more appropriate for a teen. Judy Blume's books are not as popular with readers as they were when I first became a librarian, but they still are sought out by some 'tween girls.

Many of the recent Newbery Award and honor books fit the middle school category, so some are cataloged in the children's section and some in the young adult section in many libraries; these have great 'tween appeal. Gary Schmidt's *The Wednesday Wars* is often found in the YA section; it is about a junior high student in 1967. Another great one is Joan Bauer's *Hope Was Here*. *The Graveyard Book* by Neil Gaiman, the Newbery winner in 2009, is often found in the young adult area of the library. In fact, many people find it too frightening for those under sixth grade and were surprised when it won the Newbery because they don't think of it as a "children's book." But it is very popular with 'tweens who want a "scary" book.

Some older 'tweens read books aimed at high schoolers, so it can be difficult to know where the separation is. In public libraries, it is generally accepted to let 'tweens decide for themselves if they are ready for certain teen books, especially those on sex, whereas school libraries draw a more distinct line between middle school books and high school books. Offering young adult books to 'tweens when you are doing readers' advisory may better meet their needs than will children's books. There isn't a clear answer on whether a young adult book is for 'tweens—it depends on the 'tween and on the book. Familiarize yourself with the young adult area in your library so you know which authors' works may be best suited to older 'tweens and which may be better for teens.

'Tweens Have a Wealth of Books from Which to Choose

If genre fiction doesn't seem to appeal to 'tweens after you do the readers' advisory interview, you can try other types of fiction. Maybe they would enjoy a book that has been made into a popular film. Or maybe they would prefer read-alikes (discussed in chapter 1). If you still can't find a book they like, be sure to let them look on their own. Sometimes a 'tween just needs to look at the covers of the books you mentioned and needs a little time to think without an adult nearby, which can make some 'tweens feel pressured. If all else fails, the 'tween may prefer nonfiction or graphic novels to fiction; these are discussed in upcoming chapters.

Fiction for grades four to seven includes some of the best books written for anyone! Adults can enjoy them just as much as kids, and children can learn a lot from them: emotional truths, historical facts, a sense of humor, and more. This can be the most difficult category for new librarians to learn about because there is so much; many older books don't go out of style, and the new books are published in droves. Hooking up a student with a book that helps him or her with homework is nice, but connecting a student to a novel that opens up the mind and emotions to new ideas can be groundbreaking, and nothing is more rewarding to library staff!

Helpful Books and Web Sites on 'Tween Fiction

There are several reference books that can help you find 'tween fiction. A few were mentioned in the first chapter to get you going; especially helpful are Kathleen Odean's *Great Books for Boys* and *Great Books for Girls*. Listed below are two more, as well as some Web sites.

Children's Book Awards. http://www.ucalgary.ca/~dKbrown/awards.html

An easy to use site listing children's book awards from several countries, including the United States, Canada, New Zealand, and other English-speaking countries.

Database of Award-Winning Children's Literature. http://www.dawcl.com/

Maintained by librarian Lisa R. Bartle, this handy Web site lets you search by age, type of book, and several other categories to find award-winning books for your students.

Kidsreads. http://www.kidsreads.com/series/index.asp

Very "kid friendly," this Web site lists series books, books that were made into movies, great books for boys, and plenty of other lists, reviews, and podcast booktalks to help any 'tween finding a good book to read.

Lesesne, Teri S. *Naked Reading: Uncovering What Tweens Need to Become Lifelong Readers.* Portland, ME: Stenhouse, 2006.

In one of the first books on libraries and literature to use the word *'tween*, Lesesne offers great advice on getting 'tweens to read based on her experience as a teacher.

Newbery Award and Honor Books. http://www.ala.org/ala/ mgrps/divs/alsc/awardsgrants/bookmedia/newberymedal/ newberymedal.cfm

The official homepage for the Newbery Medal, awarded by the Association of Library Service to Children, a division of the American Library Association.

Sutherland, Zena. *Children and Books.* 9th ed. New York: Longman, 1997.

Often used as a textbook for children's literature classes, Sutherland examines genre fiction and how it fulfills needs in children, such as the need to be loved. in depth.

RECOMMENDED 'TWEEN GENRE FICTION

Fantasy

Alexander, Lloyd. <u>The Chronicles of Prydain</u> series.

Babbitt, Natalie. *Tuck Everlasting.*

Baum, L. Frank. <u>The Wizard of Oz</u> series.

Black, Holly. <u>Spiderwick Chronicles</u>.

Bloor, Edward. *London Calling.*

Boston, L. M. <u>Green Knowe</u> series.

Byng, Georgia. <u>Molly Moon</u> series.

Colfer, Eoin. <u>Artemis Fowl</u> series.

Collins, Suzanne. <u>Gregor the Overlander</u> series.

Coombs, Kate. *The Runaway Princess.*

Cooper, Susan. <u>The Dark Is Rising</u> series.

Cooper, Susan. *Victory.*

DiCamillo, Kate. *Miraculous Journey of Edward Tulane.*

DiCamillo, Kate. *Tale of Despereaux.*

Duane, Diane. <u>So You Want to Be a Wizard</u> series.

DuPrau, Jeanne. *The City of Ember.*

Eager, Edward. *Half Magic.*

Funke, Cornelia. *Dragon Rider.*

Hale, Shannon. *The Goose Girl.*

Ibbotson, Eva. *The Secret of Platform Thirteen.*

Jones, Diana Wynne. *Archer's Goon.*

Juster, Norton. *Phantom Tollbooth.*

Kuijier, Guus. *Book of Everything.*

Law, Ingrid. *Savvy.*

Le Guin, Ursula. *Wizard of Earthsea.*

Lewis, C. S. *Chronicles of Narnia.*

Lindgrin, Astrid. *Pippi Longstocking.*

Lowry, Lois. *Gossamer.*

Lowry, Lois. *Messenger.*

Martin, Ann M. The Doll People series.

Martin, Rafe. *Birdwing.*

Nimmo, Jenny. The Charlie Bone series.

Norton, Mary. The Borrowers series.

Oppel, Kenneth. Silverwing series.

Paolini, Christopher. Eragon series.

Riordan, Rick. Percy Jackson series.

Rowling, J. K. Harry Potter series.

Sage, Angie. Septimus Heap series.

Seidler, Tor. *The Revenge of Randal Reese-Rat.*

Stroud, Jonathan. The Amulet of Samarkand series.

Travers, P. L. Mary Poppins series.

Wilson, N. D. 100 Cupboards series.

Winthrop, Elizabeth. Castle in the Attic series.

Wrede, Patricia. *The Thirteenth Child.*

Animal Fantasy

Avi. Poppy series.

Broach, Elise. *Masterpiece.*

Grahame, Kenneth. *The Wind in the Willows.*

Jacques, Brian. Redwall series.

King-Smith, Dick. *Babe: the Gallant Pig.*

King-Smith, Dick. *Harry's Mad.*

King-Smith, Dick. *Pretty Polly.*

King-Smith, Dick. *School Mouse.*

Seidler, Tor. *A Rat's Tale.*

Selden, George. *Cricket in Times Square.*

White, E. B. *Charlotte's Web.*

White, E. B. *Stuart Little.*

From *Readers' Advisory for Children and 'Tweens* by Penny Peck.
Santa Barbara, CA: Libraries Unlimited. Copyright © 2010.

Science Fiction

Christopher, John. <u>Tripods</u> series.

Maguire, Gregory. <u>Hamlet Chronicles</u> series.

Reeve, Philip. *Larklight: A Rousing Tale of Dauntless Pluck in the Farthest Reaches of Space.*

Service, Pamela. *Camp Alien.*

Service, Pamela. <u>Stinker from Space</u> series.

Sleator, William. *Interstellar Pig.*

Vande Velde, Vivian. *Heir Apparent.*

Waugh, Sylvia. *Earthborn.*

Waugh, Sylvia. *Space Race.*

Waugh, Sylvia. *Who Goes Home?*

Contemporary/Realistic Fiction

Baker, Deirdre. *Becca at Sea.*

Bauer, Joan. *Stand Tall.*

Birdsall, Jeanne. *The Penderwicks: A Summer Tale of Four Sisters, Two Rabbits, and a Very Interesting Boy.*

Blume, Judy. *Are You There God? It's Me, Margaret.*

Burgess, Melvin. *Kite.*

Clements, Andrew. *Frindle.*

Clements, Andrew. *The Landry News.*

Clements, Andrew. *The Last Holiday Concert.*

Clements, Andrew. *No Talking.*

Codell, Esme Raji. *Sahara Special.*

Connor, Leslie. *Waiting for Normal.*

Cottrell Boyce, Frank. *Framed.*

Couloumbis, Audrey. *Getting Near to Baby.*

Creech, Sharon. *Chasing Redbird.*

Creech, Sharon. *Ruby Holler.*

Creech, Sharon. *Walk Two Moons.*

Creech, Sharon. *The Wanderer.*

Ellis, Deborah. *I Am a Taxi.*

Ellis, Sarah. *Odd Man Out.*

Fitzhugh, Louise. *Harriet the Spy.*

Gantos, Jack. Joey Pigza series.

Gutman, Dan. *The Homework Machine.*

Henkes, Kevin. *Bird Lake Moon.*

Henkes, Kevin. *The Birthday Room.*

Henkes, Kevin. *Olive's Ocean.*

Key, Watt. *Alabama Moon.*

Kinney, Jeff. Diary of a Wimpy Kid series.

Konigsburg, E. L. *From the Mixed Up Files of Mrs. Basil E. Frankweiler.*

Konigsburg, E. L. *The Outcasts of 19 Schuyler Place.*

Konigsburg, E. L. *The View from Saturday.*

Lord, Cynthia. *Rules.*

McKay, Hilary. *Caddy Ever After.*

McKay, Hilary. *Saffy's Angel.*

Nicholls, Sally. *Ways to Live Forever.*

O'Connor, Barbara. *Me and Rupert Goody.*

Paterson, Katherine. *The Same Stuff as Stars.*

Patron, Susan. *The Higher Power of Lucky.*

Pearsall, Shelley. *All of the Above.*

Perkins, Lynne Rae. *All Alone in the Universe.*

Perkins, Lynne Rae. *Criss Cross.*

Ryan, Pamela Munoz. *Becoming Naomi Leon.*

Sanchez, Alex. *So Hard to Say.*

Stauffacher, Sue. *Harry Sue.*

Urban, Linda. *A Crooked Kind of Perfect.*

Warner, Sally. *It's Only Temporary.*

Weeks, Sarah. *So B. It.*

Wiles, Deborah. *The Aurora County All-Stars.*

Humor

Anderson, M. T. *Whales on Stilts!*

Blume, Judy. <u>Fudge</u> series.

Byars, Betsy. <u>Bingo Brown</u> series.

Byars, Betsy. <u>Blossom</u> series.

Cleary, Beverly. <u>Beezus and Ramona</u> series.

Dahl, Roald. *Charlie and the Chocolate Factory.*

Dahl, Roald. *James and the Giant Peach.*

Dahl, Roald. *Matilda.*

Feiffer, Jules. *A Barrel of Laughs, a Vale of Tears.*

Goscinny, Rene. <u>Nicholas</u> series.

Holm, Jennifer. *Middle School Is Worse Than Meatloaf: A Year Told Through Stuff.*

Klise, Katie, and M. Sarah. <u>Regarding</u> series.

Lowry, Lois. <u>Anastasia and Sam</u> series.

Paulsen, Gary. *Mudshark.*

Peck, Richard. *The Teacher's Funeral.*

Pullman, Philip. *I Was a Rat!*

Rex, Adam. *True Meaning of Smekday.*

Winkler, Henry. <u>Hank Zipzer</u> series.

Yee, Lisa. <u>Millicent Min</u> series.

Mystery/Horror/Gothic

Ardagh, Philip. <u>Eddie Dickens</u> series.

Balliett, Blue. <u>Chasing Vermeer</u> series.

Berlin, Eric. *The Puzzling World of Winston Breen.*

Broach, Elise. *Masterpiece.*

Bruchac, Joseph. <u>Skeleton Man</u> series.

Copeland, Mark. *Bundle at Blackthorpe Heath.*

Dixon, Franklin W. <u>The Hardy Boys</u> series.

Dowd, Siobhan. *The London Eye Mystery.*

Gaiman, Neil. *Coraline.*

Gaiman, Neil. *The Graveyard Book.*

Hale, Bruce. Chet Gecko series.

Ibbotson, Eva. *The Star of Kazan.*

Keene, Carolyn. Nancy Drew series.

LaFevers, R. L. Theodosia series.

Pullman, Philip. The Ruby in the Smoke series.

Snicket, Lemony. A Series of Unfortunate Events series.

Snyder, Zilpha Keatley. *The Egypt Game.*

Stewart, Trenton Lee. *The Mysterious Benedict Society.*

Stine, R. L. Goosebumps series.

Sports

Christopher, Matt. Over 100 sports fiction novels for 'tweens.

Feinstein, John. *Last Shot.*

Gutman, Dan. Million Dollar series.

Knudson, R. R. Zanballer series.

Lupica, Mike. *Heat.*

Preller, James. *Six Innings: A Game in the Life.*

Animal Stories

Burnford, Sheila. *The Incredible Journey.*

Farley, Walter. Black Stallion series.

George, Jean Craighead. *My Side of the Mountain.*

Gipson, Fred. *Old Yeller.*

Knight, Eric. *Lassie Come Home.*

Mikaelsen, Ben. *Touching Spirit Bear.*

Naylor, Phillis Reynolds. Shiloh series.

Rawls, Wilson. *Where the Red Fern Grows.*

Adventure

Avi. *The True Confessions of Charlotte Doyle.*

Hiaasen, Carl. *Hoot.*

Hiaasen, Carl. *Scat.*

Hobbs, Will. *Down the Yukon.*

Hobbs, Will. *Downriver.*

Hobbs, Will. *Far North.*

Hobbs, Will. *Go Big or Go Home.*

Lawrence, Iain. *The Castaways.*

Meyer, L. A. *Curse of the Blue Tattoo.*

Meyer, L. A. *Under the Jolly Roger.*

Paulsen, Gary. <u>Hatchet/Brian</u> series.

Pratchett, Terry. *Nation.*

Taylor, Theodore. *The Cay.*

Historical Fiction

Avi. *Crispin: The Cross of Lead.*

Avi. *Crispin at the Edge of the World.*

Blackwood, Gary L. *Moonshine.*

Blackwood, Gary L. *Shakespeare Stealer.*

Bredsdorff, Bodil. *The Crow-Girl.*

Choldenko, Gennifer. *Al Capone Does My Shirts.*

Choldenko, Gennifer. *Al Capone Shines My Shoes.*

Curtis, Christopher Paul. *Bud, Not Buddy.*

Curtis, Christopher Paul. *Elijah of Buxton.*

Cushman, Karen. *The Ballad of Lucy Whipple.*

Cushman, Karen. *Catherine Called Birdy.*

Cushman, Karen. *The Loud Silence of Francine Green.*

Cushman, Karen. *Matilda Bone.*

Cushman, Karen. *The Midwife's Apprentice.*

Cushman, Karen. *Rodzina.*

Erdrich, Louise. *Birchbark House* series.

Farmer, Nancy. *The Sea of Trolls.*

Gerstein, Mordicai. *The Old Country.*

Giff, Patricia Reilly. *Maggie's Door.*

Giff, Patricia Reilly. *Nory Ryan's Song.*

Hertenstein, Jane. *Beyond Paradise.*

Hesse, Karen. *Out of the Dust.*

Hesse, Karen. *Witness.*

Holm, Jennifer L. *Penny from Heaven.*

Hoobler, Dorothy, and Thomas Hoobler. *In Darkness, Death.*

Ibbotson, Eva. *The Dragonfly Pool.*

Kadohata, Cynthia. *Weedflower.*

Klages, Ellen. *The Green Glass Sea.*

Larson, Kirby. *Hattie Big Sky.*

Lisle, Janet Taylor. *Black Duck.*

Martin, Ann M. *A Corner of the Universe.*

McCaughrean, Geraldine. *The Kite Rider.*

Napoli, Donna Jo. *The King of Mulberry Street.*

O'Dell, Scott. *Island of the Blue Dolphins.*

Peck, Richard. *A Long Way from Chicago.*

Peck, Richard. *The River Between Us.*

Schmidt, Gary D. *Lizzie Bright and the Buckminster Boy.*

Schmidt, Gary D. *The Wednesday Wars.*

Sedgwick, Marcus. *My Swordhand Is Singing.*

Selznick, Brian. *The Invention of Hugo Cabret.*

Sherlock, Patti. *Letters from Wolfie.*

Sturtevant, Katherine. *A True and Faithful Narrative.*

Sturtevant, Katherine. *At the Sign of the Star.*

Taylor, Mildred D. *Roll of Thunder Hear My Cry.*

Turnbull, Ann. *No Shame, No Fear.*

Wells, Rosemary. *Red Moon at Sharpsburg.*

Yep, Laurence. <u>Gold Mountain Chronicles</u> series.

Yolen, Jane. *The Devil's Arithmetic.*

Chapter 7

Multicultural Books for Children and 'Tweens

Books are mirrors in which children see themselves, as well as windows onto the world of diverse perspectives and experiences. To meet the needs of the diverse children and families they serve, libraries provide books by multicultural authors and illustrators. The literary mirrors and windows provided must frame believable characters, authentic language, and historically accurate or realistic plots.

Multicultural Fiction

It is worth noting that books representing a certain culture are not just for children from that culture. If it is a good book, it is for everyone. In some areas of the United States and Canada, many children may not have a classmate who is Asian American, or African American, and those children need to read about their experiences to help prepare them for our increasingly multicultural society. So when you are doing readers' advisory, it is important to offer these books to all children, not just to those from that culture (which would be a form of ethnic profiling).

Prior to 1969 and the publication of *Stevie* by John Steptoe, a child of color was infrequently seen in children's picture books, the notable exceptions being picture books by Don Freeman (*Corduroy*), Leo Politi, and Ezra Jack Keats, who depicted children of color even though they were European American. In chapter books the absence of African American, Latino, Native American Indian, and other multicultural characters was even more striking. Beginning in the late 1960s, books by African American authors Virginia Hamilton, Mildred Taylor, and Walter Dean Myers started to emerge. Yoshiko Uchida wrote stories from the Japanese American experience on the West Coast, and Bette Bao Lord wrote about the Chinese American experience on the East Coast. But these were still exceptions to the rule. Fortunately the civil rights movement opened doors for authors and illustrators of various cultural backgrounds to be published in the 1970s and beyond. Libraries' bookshelves have been enriched by this diversity of authors.

African American Fiction

There is a rich heritage of African American children's books, in part due to the promotion provided by the Coretta Scott King book award (see below). Many children's and 'tweens' books feature African American poetry, folklore, and history, and there are wonderful picture books and novels by African American writers. Leo Dillon and Diane Dillon write and illustrate wonderful books, as do Jerry Pinkney and many of his family members, including Brian Pinkney and Andrea Davis Pinkney. Other great African American picture book authors and illustrators include Kadir Nelson, E. B. Lewis, Bryan Collier, and Patricia McKissack.

In the world of 'tween books, Jacqueline Woodson has won several awards, including Newbery honor citations for her realistic novels for 'tweens. Other successful African American authors for 'tweens are Christopher Paul Curtis (a Newbery winner), Nikki Grimes, Angela Johnson, Joyce Carol Thomas, and Karen English.

Urban Fiction

One area of multicultural fiction that is not exclusively African American, but is often from that culture, is urban fiction (sometimes called street lit). These dramatic novels are filled with raw depictions of life in the inner city, which at times includes sex, drugs, and violence. Generally, urban fiction is for adults and older high school students. But there are a few 'tween novels that have urban fiction elements and are age appropriate for older 'tweens.

A popular paperback series is <u>Bluford High</u>, written by Paul Langan and other authors; these books include plots focusing on school life in the inner city, but tone down the sex and swearing while still giving readers the drama they are seeking. Other 'tween-appropriate books with urban fiction elements include Jacqueline Woodson's *The First Part Last*, Sharon Flake's *Begging for Change,* and Janet McDonald's *Spellbound*. When assisting a 'tween who is asking for urban fiction, it can be difficult to discern if a book will be too "adult" for that 'tween. On the other hand, we don't want to be censors. There are several Web sites listed at the end of this chapter that offer reviews of urban fiction. For more on urban fiction for 'tweens, check out the reviews in *School Library Journal* and *VOYA: Voice of Youth Advocates.*

Asian American Fiction

Notable authors of Asian American fiction for children and 'tweens include Newbery Award recipients Laurence Yep, Linda Sue Park, and Cynthia Kadohata, who all write wonderful 'tween novels. Caldecott Medalists include Ed Young and Allen Say. Other Asian American picture book creators include Rosanne Thong, Huy Voun Lee, Lenore Look, Grace Lin, and Taro Gomi. The publisher Lee and Low specializes in multicultural children's books, including many from the Asian American experience. There is no national award for children's Asian American fiction, like the Coretta Scott King Award for African American children's books or the Pura Belpre Award for Latino/Hispanic children's books, but there are enough great writers from Asian backgrounds to warrant one.

Native American Fiction

Although there are not as many published Native American children's authors as there is demand for, some are receiving great reviews, and their books are increasingly found in classrooms and public libraries. These authors include Joseph Bruchac, a renowned Abenaki storyteller; Louise Erdrich, known for her adult novels and poetry, who has written three children's novels featuring a young Ojibwe girl named Omakayas; and Cynthia Leitich Smith, a member of the Muskogee (Creek) nation, whose books are about contemporary Native American children. Native American picture book illustrators include Shonto

Begay. Alexie Sherman is an award-winning author of teen books; perhaps he will write for 'tweens as well. For more on Native American children's books, look at the recommendations at www.Oyate.org. Oyate is a nonprofit organization dedicated to promoting children's books that accurately depict Native American cultures.

Latino/Hispanic Fiction

The Latino population is currently the fastest growing ethnic group in the United States, but the children's book business hasn't yet caught up with that fact. There are some notable authors with Latino backgrounds, representing primarily Mexican American, Cuban American, and Puerto Rican cultures. On the West Coast, Gary Soto has written several successful 'tween novels. Francisco Jimenez has written autobiographical novels on the migrant worker experience. And David Diaz, a Caldecott Medal illustrator, has done several picture books. Pamela Muñoz Ryan sets many of her books in California, where she grew up. Alma Flor Ada writes about her childhood in Cuba. On the East Coast, noted photographer George Ancona has written several children's books, both nonfiction and fiction. There are also successful poets who write for children, including Pat Mora and Francisco X. Alarcon.

There are a few popular Latino picture book illustrators; hopefully more will get published as the book industry realizes what a big market there is for this group. Look for picture books by Lulu Delacre, Lucia M. Gonzalez, Yuyi Morales, and Joe Cepeda.

Publishers that specialize in Latino/Hispanic books for children include Piñata Books and Children's Book Press (which publishes books from other cultures as well). Piñata Books is part of Arte Publico Press, which is part of the University of Houston, Texas. Children's Book Press is a nonprofit publisher that focuses on Pacific Rim cultures. Either publisher can be a great resource if you are thinking about adding more Latino and multicultural children's books to your collection.

Multicultural Nonfiction

Of course multicultural nonfiction is important to the school curriculum, especially for social studies. But many children and 'tweens enjoy nonfiction, including multicultural nonfiction, for recreational reading. For example, they may enjoy the history of the country from which a grandparent emigrated to the United States. Or they may want to learn about a cultural group in the United States. Using the online catalog should be the easiest way to find books on any multicultural nonfiction topic, from origami to tae kwon do to the Negro Baseball Leagues to jazz music.

A key nonfiction topic that may appeal to a wide range of readers is biography, of both historical and contemporary figures. Often these will be great artists or leaders from a specific culture. There are both picture book and 'tween biographies about many different people, both the well-known and the lesser known. Of course there are plenty of books on figures like Barack Obama, Cesar Chavez, Rosa Parks, and Martin Luther King Jr. But also seek out biographies of less well-known people like Chinese American actress Anna May Wong (*Shining Star* by Paula Yoo) or the Latino labor leader Jessie de la Cruz (*Jessie de La Cruz: A Profile of a United Farm Worker* by Gary Soto). Browse biographies to find books on people you may not have heard about, or whom the children may not know about, and acquire some newer biographies on contemporary multicultural figures, from Tiger Woods to Lucy Liu.

Promoting Multicultural Fiction

One way to promote multicultural fiction is to include it whenever you are doing readers' advisory; for example, offer Christopher Paul Curtis's *Bud Not Buddy* when a 'tween is looking for historical fiction. Or recommend Laurence Yep's *Cockroach Cooties* to the 'tween who enjoys mysteries. But you can also promote multicultural fiction in less labor-intensive ways than the hand-selling done during readers' advisory.

It is generally thought that multicultural fiction should not be separated from regular juvenile fiction because it "ghettoizes" the books. But you can help the casual browser find books by authors of certain cultures with simple labels that are commercially purchased, the way genre labels are used. There are labels for Latino, Asian, African American, and Native American that fit on the spine of a book, just like a genre label. Parents, teachers, and 'tweens can tell at a glance if a book is written by someone from that culture. This can be helpful for book report assignments, as some teachers ask students to read a book by an author of a certain culture for a specific celebration.

Booklists celebrating specific cultures are also helpful. These can be easier for parents and teachers to use than searching the online catalog, and very often adults request multicultural books for children and 'tweens. The lists can be especially useful during certain times of year when the public is seeking books on a specific culture, such as Latino books for a Cinco de Mayo celebration.

Book displays can also promote multicultural literature. Many minority authors understand that having such displays for certain cultural celebrations is natural, but they want their books to be highlighted at other times of the year as well. For example, you might do an African American literature display for Black History month, but you could also do one in August to coincide with Barack Obama's birthday, since he is the first African American president. Or create a display of Hawaii-related children's books for Obama's birthday, since he was born in Hawaii.

Other Cultural Groups

There are many other cultural groups in the United States. For example, in the Asian American category, you could focus on Chinese American books for the Lunar New Year, or Japanese American books in May for Pacific Heritage Month, or Filipino books in October for Filipino American History Month. There is also a rich history of children's books from the Jewish perspective; books celebrating Arab and other Middle Eastern groups; as well as books on what it is like to be Italian American, Polish American, Irish American, and so forth. In some communities, a dominant cultural group may even help you prepare a display.

Book Awards

As discussed in chapter 6, the Newbery is far and away the best known book award for a children's book. But there are some awards that focus on distinguished children's books by authors of specific ethnicities.

Coretta Scott King Award

In 1975 Virginia Hamilton was awarded the Newbery for *M.C. Higgins the Great*, and in 1977, Mildred Taylor won for *Roll of Thunder, Hear My Cry*. But in 1969 many people were tired of waiting for some acknowledgment of the contributions of African American authors and illustrators to children's literature. So African American librarians started the Coretta Scott King Awards, with criteria similar to those of the Newbery and Caldecott, to award excellence in children's literature by African Americans. In 1999 *Bud Not Buddy* by Christopher Paul Curtis was the first children's book to receive both the Newbery Medal and Coretta Scott King Award. As of this writing, Jerry Pinkney and Leo

Dillon are the only African Americans who have received the Caldecott Medal, so there is arguably still a need for this award. The Coretta Scott King Awards are administered by the American Library Association. Many school and public libraries use the yearly winners and honor books to build up their African American children's book collections.

Pura Belpre Award

Pura Belpre was a storyteller and librarian at the New York Public Library in the 1920s, 1930s, and 1940s. Originally from Puerto Rico, she did outreach to the Spanish-speaking community of the city to show them the library had something to offer them. The Pura Belpre Award is named after her; it was started in 1996 to award Latino/Hispanic authors of children's books published in the United States. From 1996 to 2008, it was given every other year. Now the award is given annually to an author and an illustrator, with honor books also named, similar to the Coretta Scott King Awards.

Other Awards

The Sydney Taylor Award is given annually to a book for youth that accurately depicts the Jewish experience. It is named after the author of the All of a Kind Family series. The Association of Jewish Libraries presents the award in three categories: teen, older readers, and younger readers. Like many other book awards, there is a gold medalist, and the honor books win the silver. For more information, go to www.jewishlibraries.org.

As mentioned above, there is no award yet for Asian American children's books. But there may come a day when that occurs, as these awards help promote multicultural books. Many librarians will use these annual award lists for collection development, to ensure that they have the best books from these cultures.

Offering Multicultural Fiction to All

As stated at the beginning of this chapter, it is important that multicultural books be included when doing readers' advisory for anyone. All readers, not just African Americans, can enjoy Bill Cosby's Little Bill easy readers; and Bud, Not Buddy is popular with fifth graders of all cultures. Use the lists at the end of the chapter for special cultural celebrations, displays, and programs, as well as offering them whenever a child or 'tween is just looking for "a good book." Multicultural fiction can speak to all of us with great writing and interesting facts and stories, so don't just offer it when it is specifically requested. These books are great all year long!

Helpful Books and Web Sites on Multicultural Fiction

There are several books and Web sites that can help you find multi-cultural children's books, in part because teachers request these so frequently. Following are just a few to get you started in finding great multicultural books for youth:

Ada, Alma Flor. *A Magical Encounter: Latino Children's Literature in the Classroom.* 2nd ed. Boston: Allyn and Bacon, 2003.

Cuban American author and education professor Alma Flor Ada lists a wealth of Latino books for children and describes how to use them in classroom situations.

Association of Jewish Libraries. www.jewishlibraries.org

Click on "Awards," and check out the authors and titles of the Sydney Taylor award books, given for children's books with Jewish content.

Coretta Scott King Award. http://www.ala.org/ala/mgrps/rts/emiert/cskbookawards/index.cfm

The Web site for the Coretta Scott King Award, named after the wife of Martin Luther King Jr., to honor African American authors and illustrators of books for children.

Day, Frances Ann. *Latina and Latino Voices in Literature: Lives and Works Updated and Expanded.* Santa Barbara, CA: Greenwood Press, 2003.

Thirty-five Latino authors and illustrators of books for youth are profiled; includes booklists.

Oyate. www.oyate.org

Oyate is a nonprofit organization that evaluates Native American books for authenticity. Its Web site has a catalog of books, divided into grade levels, found to be authentic. The site also has a list of books to avoid.

Pura Belpre Award. http://www.ala.org/ala/mgrps/divs/alsc/ awardsgrants/bookmedia/belpremedal/index.cfm

The Web site of the Pura Belpre Award, given for the best children's books from Latino/Hispanic authors and illustrators.

Rand, Donna, Toni Trent Parker, and Sheila Foster. *Black Books Galore! Guide to Great African American Children's Books.* New York: John Wiley & Sons, 1998.

Aimed at parents, this useful guide lists more than 500 books, arranged by age groups. There is also a follow-up book, *Black Books Galore! Guide to More Great African American Children's Books*, released in 2001.

Smith, Henrietta M. *The Coretta Scott King Awards, 1970-2009: 40th Anniversary.* Chicago: American Library Association, 2009.

Smith describes firsthand how the awards were devised and then lists all the winner and honor books. Also included are brief biographies of the authors and illustrators.

Urban Fiction for Tweens. http://www.libsuccess.org/ index. php?title=My_Favorite_Urban_Fiction_Titles_for_ Teens%2C_from_Miranda_Doyle%2C_San_Francisco

Compiled by middle school librarian Miranda Doyle, this is a list of young adult novels with urban fiction elements that may be requested by some older 'tweens.

Urban Fiction from the Redford Library. http://www. redfordlibrary.org/pdf_files/teen_urban.pdf

A list of urban fiction for 'tweens and teens, recommended by the Redford Library in Michigan.

CHILDREN'S MULTICULTURAL FICTION

African American Books for Younger Readers

Adoff, Arnold. *Black Is Brown Is Tan.*

Aston, Dianna Hutts. *The Moon Over Star.*

Barbour, Karen. *Mr. Williams.*

Chocolate, Deborah. *On the Day I Was Born.*

Clifton, Lucille. <u>Everett Anderson</u> series.

Collier, Bryan. *Uptown.*

Johnson, Angela. *Julius.*

Lester, Julius. *John Henry.*

Manning, Maurie J. *Kitchen Dance.*

McKissack, Patricia. *Goin' Someplace Special.*

Myers, Christopher. *Black Cat.*

Pinkney, Sandra. *A Rainbow All Around Me.*

Ringgold, Faith. *Tar Beach.*

Steptoe, John. *Mufaro's Beautiful Daughters.*

Weatherford, Carole Boston. *Before John Was a Jazz Giant: A Song of John Coltrane.*

Weatherford, Carole Boston. *Freedom on the Menu.*

Weatherford, Carole Boston. *Moses: When Harriet Tubman Led Her People to Freedom.*

Winter, Jonah. *Dizzy.*

Woodson, Jacqueline. *Show Way.*

Asian American Books for Younger Readers

Bridges, Shirin Yim. *Ruby's Wish.*

Chinn, Karen. *Sam and the Lucky Money.*

Choi, Yansook. *New Cat.*

Lee, Huy Voun. *At the Beach.*

Lee, Milly. *Landed.*

Nakagawa, Chihiro. *Who Made This Cake?*

Nyeu, Tao. *Wonder Bear.*

Park, Frances and Ginger. *The Have a Good Day Cafe.*

Pham, LeUyen. *Big Sister, Little Sister.*

Recorvits, Helen. *My Name Is Yoon.*

Say, Allen. *Grandfather's Journey.*

Thong, Roseanne. *Red Is a Dragon: A Book of Colors.*

Yamate, Sandra. *Ashok by Any Other Name.*

Yi, Hu Yong. *Good Morning China.*

Young, Ed. *Lon Po Po: A Red Riding Story from China.*

Native American Books for Younger Readers

Archambault, John. *Knots on a Counting Rope.*

Harjo, Joy. *The Good Luck Cat.*

Joosse, Barbara M. *Mama Do You Love Me?*

McCain, Becky Ray. *Grandmother's Dreamcatcher.*

Smith, Cynthia Leitich. *Jingle Dancer.*

Latino/Hispanic Books for Younger Readers

Ada, Alma Flor. *Pio Peep! Traditional Spanish Nursery Rhymes.*

Ancona, George. *Fiesta Fireworks.*

Brown, Monica. *My Name Is Gabito: The Life of Gabriel Marques.*

Delacre, Lulu. *Arroz Con Leche: Popular Songs and Rhymes from Latin America.*

Dorros, Arthur. *Abuela.*

Dorros, Arthur. *Papa and Me.*

Elya, Susan M. *Bebe Goes Shopping.*

Gonzalez, Lucia. *The Bossy Gallito.*

Gonzalez, Lucia. *The Storyteller's Candle.*

Montes, Marisa. *Los Gatos Black on Halloween.*

Mora, Pat. *Dona Flor: A Tall Tale about a Giant Woman with a Big Heart.*

Morales, Yuyi. *Little Night.*

Ryan, Pamela Muñoz. *Mice and Beans.*

Shahan, Sherry. *Spicy Hot Colors.*

Smith, J. D. *The Best Mariachi in the World.*

Soto, Gary. *Chato's Kitchen.*

Soto, Gary. *My Little Car.*

Tafolla, Carmen. *What Can You Do with a Rebozo?*

Jewish Books for Younger Readers

Hesse, Karen. *The Cats in Krasinski Square.*

Levinson, Riki. *Soon, Annala.*

Littlesugar, Amy. *Willy and Max: A Holocaust Story.*

Polacco, Patricia. *The Keeping Quilt.*

Schur, Maxine Rose. *The Peddler's Gift.*

Taback, Simms. *Joseph Had a Little Overcoat.*

Taylor, Sydney. All of a Kind Family series.

Wing, Natasha. *Jalapeno Bagels.*

Yolen, Jane. *Naming Liberty.*

Zemach, Margot. *It Could Always Be Worse: A Yiddish Folktale.*

Middle Eastern Books for Younger Readers

Addasi, Maha. *The White Nights of Ramadan.*

Balouch, Kristen. *Mystery Bottle.*

Heide, Florence Parry. *The Day of Ahmed's Secret.*

Heide, Florence Parry. *Sami and the Times of Troubles.*

Lewin, Betsy. *What's the Matter, Habibi?*

Modin-Uddin, Asma. *My Name Is Bilal.*

Nye, Naomi Shihab. *Sitti's Secrets.*

Rumford, James. *Silent Music: A Story of Baghdad.*

Williams, Karen Lynn. *Four Feet, Two Sandals.*

'TWEEN MULTICULTURAL FICTION

African American 'Tween Books

Curtis, Christopher Paul. *Bud, Not Buddy.*

Curtis, Christopher Paul. *Elijah of Buxton.*

Curtis, Christopher Paul. *The Watsons Go to Birmingham—1963.*

Elliott, Zetta. *Bird.*

English, Karen. *Francie.*

Hamilton, Virginia. *The House of Dies Drear.*

Hamilton, Virginia. *M.C Higgins the Great.*

Hansen, Joyce. *I Thought My Soul Would Rise and Fly.*

Johnson, Angela. *Heaven.*

Lester, Julius. *Days of Tears: A Novel in Dialogue.*

Moses, Sheila P. *The Legend of Buddy Bush.*

Smith, Hope Anita. *Keeping the Night Watch.*

Taylor, Mildred. *The Land.*

Taylor, Mildred D. <u>Roll of Thunder Hear My Cry</u> series.

Woodson, Jacqueline. *After Tupac and D Foster.*

Woodson, Jacqueline. *Feathers.*

Woodson, Jacqueline. *Locomotion.*

Asian American 'Tween Books

Compestine, Ying Chang. *Revolution Is Not a Dinner Party.*

Himelblau, Linda. *The Trouble Begins.*

Kadohata, Cynthia. *Outside Beauty.*

Kadohata, Cynthia. *Weedflower.*

Lin, Grace. *The Year of the Dog.*

Look, Lenore. <u>Alvin Ho Series</u>.

Look, Lenore. <u>Ruby Lu</u> series.

Lord, Bette Bao. *In the Year of the Boar and Jackie Robinson.*

Namioka, Lensey. *Ties That Bind, Ties That Break.*

Namioka, Lensey. *Yang the Youngest and His Terrible Ear.*

Park, Linda Sue. *My Name Was Keoko.*

Park, Linda Sue. *A Single Shard.*

Perkins, Mitali. *Monsoon Summer.*

Singh, Vandana. *Younguncle Comes to Town.*

Uchida, Yoshiko. *A Jar of Dreams.*

Yep, Laurence. Gold Mountain Chronicles series.

Yep, Laurence. *Ribbons.*

Native American 'Tween Books

Alexie, Sherman. *The Absolutely True Story of a Part-time Indian.*

Bruchac, Joseph. *Bearwalker.*

Bruchac, Joseph. *Skeleton Man.*

Carvell, Marlene. *Sweetgrass Basket.*

Creech, Sharon. *Walk Two Moons.*

Erdich, Louise. *The Birchback House* series.

George, Jean Craighead. *Julie of the Wolves.*

Hill, Kirkpatrick. *The Year of Miss Agnes.*

Smith, Cynthia Leitich. *Indian Shoes.*

Smith, Cynthia Leitich. *Rain Is Not My Indian Name.*

Latino/Hispanic Tween Books

Alvarez, Julia. *Before We Were Free.*

Engle, Margarita. *The Surrender Tree: Poems of Cuba's Struggle for Freedom.*

Jimenez, Francisco. The Circuit series.

Johnston, Tony. *Any Small Goodness.*

Resau, Laura. *What the Moon Saw.*

Ryan, Pamela Muñoz. *Becoming Naomi Leon.*

Ryan, Pamela Muñoz. *Esperanza Rising.*

Soto, Gary. *Summer on Wheels.*

Jewish 'Tween Books

Codell, Esme Raji. *Vive La Paris.*

Glatshteyn, Yankev. *Emil and Karl.*

Herman, Charlotte. *My Chocolate Year.*

Isaacs, Anne. *Torn Thread.*

Konigsburg, E. L. *About the B'nai Bagels.*

Lowry, Lois. *Number the Stars.*

Matas, Carol. *Daniel's Story.*

Orlev, Uri. *Island on Bird Street.*

Orlev, Uri. *Run, Boy, Run.*

Roy, Jennifer. *Yellow Star.*

Sachs, Marilyn. *Lost in America.*

Schnur, Steven. *The Koufax Dilemma.*

Middle Eastern 'Tween Books

Barakat, Ibtisam. *Tasting the Sky: A Palestinian Childhood.*

Budhos, Marina. *Ask Me No Questions.*

Ellis, Deborah. *The Breadwinner.*

Fletcher, Susan. *Shadow Spinner.*

O'Brien, Tony, and Mike Sullivan. *Afghan Dreams: Young Voices of Afghanistan.*

Chapter 8

Nonfiction Books for Recreational Reading

In both public and school libraries, nonfiction or informational books are heavily used, for several reasons. First, many students need resources for homework: books for state reports, how-to books with science experiments, books on social issues for debates, and much more. Second, parents and children use nonfiction books relevant to issues in their lives, like a new adopted sibling, a health concern, and so forth. Third, teachers use children's nonfiction books in the classroom to expand on or even substitute for material that may not be in the textbook, or that may be out of date in the textbook. Fourth, children (and adults) enjoy nonfiction books that give them ideas for arts and crafts, games and sports, celebrations and holidays, and other hands-on activities. Finally, many readers of all ages like nonfiction books for recreational reading, from dinosaur books to fascinating biographies and history.

Nonfiction Series

Often nonfiction books for young readers are published in series, which means that they are very useful for homework, but are not fascinating, compelling reading. This doesn't mean these books are bad; in fact, they are often nicely composed, with interesting photos or other book design elements, and have clear texts that convey the information. If they are accurate and useful, rise above the pedestrian, and are not boring, these books have a rightful place on the library shelf. For example, Chelsea House is well respected for several of its series, such as <u>Black Americans of Achievement</u>. Coretta Scott King Award winners and honorees have written some of the books in this series, and the wealth of photos and other design elements make these books stand out. Often children enjoy those series books that are on subjects they're interested in for recreational reading. Another popular nonfiction series is <u>Eyewitness</u> from DK Publishers; children pore over the color photos in these books.

Narrative Nonfiction

Many adult nonfiction best-seller lists include books that teach how to invest money, create fabulous meals, or live a purpose-driven life. But there is also a wealth of "narrative nonfiction," books that tell the story of a life, of something in history, or other true story that is so entertaining it reads like fiction. For example, the life of the racehorse Seabiscuit was on the *New York Times* Adult Nonfiction Bestseller List for years before being made into a hit film. These aren't instructional books, but rather fascinating true events woven into a narrative that reads like the most compelling novel. There are many examples of narrative nonfiction for children as well; refer to the annual ALA/ALSC Notable Children's Books lists at http://www.ala.org/ala/mgrps/divs/alsc/awardsgrants/childrensnotable/notablechibooks/index.cfm. From Catherine Thimmesh's *Team Moon: How 400,00 People Landed Apollo 11 on the Moon*, to Jennifer Armstrong's tale of Shackleton's Antarctic adventure in *Shipwreck at the Bottom of the World*, to John Fleischman's *Phineas Gage: A Gruesome but True Story about Brain Science*, children's nonfiction includes many examples of narrative nonfiction. The books tell true stories, but they also have amazing characters, page-turning chapters, and a lot of drama. Best of all, these books often reach children who don't gravitate to fiction.

Nonfiction Book Design

Due to most children's sophisticated visual literacy, the demand for superior book design in children's informational books is high. Children look for abundant color photos, sidebars, reproductions of illustrations from the time period, pleasingly large typefaces and interesting borders and other page decorations, and all manner of other graphic elements that add visual interest to a nonfiction book. A nonfiction book for children almost needs to look like a coffee-table book. Of course, the book design should be appropriate for the topic and the audience. For example, Joy Cowley's *Red-Eyed Tree Frog* is aimed at the primary grades, so the typeface is large, and the color photos are clear and glowing. The background pages and borders vary in shades of green, similar to the frog's actual environment. The book is very striking and visually pleasing. Other examples are Jan Greenberg's and Sandra Jordan's biographies of artist Chuck Close and architect Frank O. Gehry; both books have an "edge" that indicates these are modern, creative people.

Book design is also important in instructional books like cookbooks or science experiment books; the best books have step-by-step instructions that appear both as a photo or diagram and in text form, so that the reader can be sure of following the instructions as accurately as possible. Of course books illustrated with photos of people should represent all races and both genders; a how-to book on basketball should not just show boys, and a cookbook should not just show girls. Likewise, a science experiment book should show that not just one ethnic group is interested in science.

Pop-Up and Toy Nonfiction

A recent popular series of nonfiction books published by Candlewick includes titles such as *Dragonology*, *Egyptology*, and *Pirateology*. These books contain little pop-ups, envelopes with letters, puzzles, and other three-dimensional elements that add a "treasure hunt" aspect to the book design. These are very popular with a wide age range and may be the type of informational books kids expect to find in a library. They take a fascinating subject and use both the illustrations and the text to make it even more engrossing. Other publishers have noted the success of this series and are also publishing three-dimensional nonfiction books, including *A Knight's City* by Philip Steele, *Robots* by Clive Gifford, and *Pyramids and Mummies* by Anne Bolton. All of these pop-up books contain information a student could use for a report, and the moveable elements hold the attention of a reluctant reader.

Informational/nonfiction books are best when the texts are as compelling as the best fiction, and the book design is of the quality of a coffee-table book. These books are useful for homework but are also very entertaining reading, and can help a child with his or her need to know. Often nonfiction is the only type of book some 'tweens will read, especially boys, who just don't like fiction. Offer them photo-filled books on subjects they are interested in. They also often enjoy books with riddles and jokes, or with lists of facts, such as *The Guinness Book of World Records*.

Backmatter and Documentation

In the past, it was taken for granted that a nonfiction book was accurate. However, some books, even a few award winners, have been found to contain factual errors. Now librarians need to be on the lookout for mistakes in nonfiction books, from science experiments that don't "work," to factual errors in history books, to unattributed quotations that the subject never actually said, to assumptions that go beyond conjecture to just "guessing."

For example, a recent book on the California Gold Rush of 1849 uses quotes from Chinese immigrants housed on Angel Island, but Angel Island wasn't used as an immigration center until 1910. It is important to check source notes in nonfiction books, so you can further research where a quote originated, where a photo was taken from from, and so forth. Ideally, the book's backmatter should include an index, a glossary if needed, a list of further reading for the same grade level, a list of resources used by the author, and a list of Web sites if relevant; the more documentation, the better.

Related to documentation is the need for up-to-date material; that is why we "weed" nonfiction books more frequently than fiction. From straight facts, such as new information on astronomy, to modern ideas on race and culture, nonfiction books should reflect the ideas and knowledge of our time, not of past eras. There are a few exceptions, of course, but even a children's book on Thomas Jefferson should portray him not only as a Founding Father who espoused "liberty and justice for all," but also as a conflicted slave-owner.

Sibert Award

Like the Newbery, the Sibert Award considers several factors when bestowing the prize for best children's informational book. Just ten years old, the Sibert is already greatly respected in the library community. The first recipient was Marc Aronson for his book on Sir Walter Raleigh. Aronson is best known as an editor, not a writer; he edited Judd Winick's *Pedro and Me*, which was a runner up the year Aronson won the Sibert! A few years ago Bartoletti's *Black Potatoes* won. Both winners were thoughtful histories that are well-documented and wonderfully designed, with abundant illustrations, many reproductions from the time period. Another favorite Sibert winner is *Team Moon: How 400,000 People Landed Apollo 11 on the Moon* by Catherine Thimmesh.

The Sibert was founded because the Newbery didn't often seem to consider nonfiction as "award" material. Milton Meltzer, who cowrote the first African American history book for children with Langston Hughes *A Pictorial History of the Negro in America*, wrote an editorial in *Horn Book* magazine in 1976, making the case that nonfiction was award-worthy but ignored. The Newbery committee did name a nonfiction book as an honor book occasionally, and Russell Freedman won the Newbery for his photobiography of Lincoln. In the past, the Newbery committee members may not have considered nonfiction as writing that was a passion for the author, so nonfiction works rarely received Newbery recognition. The dramatic texts found in narrative nonfiction have changed that perception. The Sibert and Newbery committees take nonfiction writing seriously and think of it as awardworthy. The idea of narrative nonfiction is relatively new; in fact, it is almost "trendy" right now. Look for these high-quality, engaging nonfiction books when doing readers' advisory.

Biography

Biography may be the most popular part of your nonfiction collection. Students are often introduced to biography in the primary grades, where they learn about people like Dr. Martin Luther King Jr., George Washington, Abraham Lincoln, Cesar Chavez, Rosa Parks, and other icons. Then, in the fourth and fifth grades, when social studies becomes such a large part of the curriculum, they read full-length biographies. Many teachers assign biographies for book reports; sometimes even having the children dress up like the people they read about. In the history of children's literature, biography became very popular with a series from the publisher Bobbs-Merrill, which began in 1932. This series focused on the childhoods of great American heroes; however, the books were very heavily fictionalized, with invented dialogue and events. Most libraries no longer carry these due to their inaccuracies, but many of us over forty (and even some younger) remember finding these light orange book jackets and reading the books over and over.

Picture Book Biographies

In the past decade there has been a big increase in picture book biographies. Some, like Andrea Pinkney and Brian Pinkney's book on Duke Ellington, focus on a person the average primary grader hasn't heard of, but will enjoy learning about. Some are brief but memorable, and visually distinctive, like *Malcolm X: A Fire Burning Brightly* by Walter Dean Myers, illustrated by Leonard Jenkins. Many students who would normally feel "too old" for picture books (like 'tweens) enjoy these books because they know the subject and find them easier to read than standard biographies. Diane Stanley has created several notable picture book biographies, and David Adler (author of the Cam Jansen mysteries) has written a whole series of picture book biographies. There is a wealth of these wonderful biographies, and even though they are in a picture book format, they should still meet the nonfiction standards of accuracy, documentation, footnotes, bibliography, and other features.

Accuracy in Biographies

Recent *New York Times* adult best-seller lists included a biography of Andrew Jackson, and another on FDR, and celebrity biographies are always big sellers. The popularity of biography begins when readers are first introduced to it and seems to continue into adulthood, especially if the biography has storytelling elements and an attractive book design. Of course, a biography should not contain invented dialogue or inaccuracies. Some conjecture is allowable if the text clearly states that "our hero may have done such and such" rather than "our hero did such and such." Another common problem, usually in biographies for the primary grades, is referring to a subject by his or her first name, such as stating "Little Martin did" about Dr. Martin Luther King Jr. As a child he was called Mike, not Martin, so this would be both inaccurate and overly familiar!

Popular Authors of Biographies

A popular biographer for young people is Russell Freedman, who often includes a wealth of photos in his books. His books on Martha Graham, Marian Anderson, and Babe Didrikson Zaharias are exciting, even to those who didn't know very much about the subjects to begin with. Similar in style are books by Elizabeth Partridge, whose first biography was on Dorothea Lange, the noted Depression Era photographer. Partridge's biography on Woody Guthrie received rave reviews, and she also wrote a biography on John Lennon. Jean Fritz (*Bully for You, Teddy*

Roosevelt!) and James Cross Giblin (*The Amazing Life of Benjamin Franklin*) have also written several wonderful biographies. Laurie Lawlor is a newer biographer, whose book on Helen Keller was refreshingly frank and well designed, with lots of photos. Judith Fradin and Dennis Fradin have also written several thorough, well-documented biographies that feature a wealth of photos.

Evaluating Biographies

When evaluating biography, consider several criteria. Of course, look for authenticity; is the book truthful and accurate, are quotations documented, and are photos relevant? Is it objective; are both the person's flaws and achievements included? Or is it hagiography, only focusing on the positive attributes of its subject? Is the book well designed, with photos or reproductions of period artwork, like Sue Macy's *Bull's Eye: A Photobiography of Annie Oakley*? If it is a collective biography, do the people included have something in common, and is it clear when each person lived, as it is in Kathleen Krull's *Lives of the Artists: Masterpieces, Messes (and What the Neighbors Thought)*? Does the writer tell you what the subject was thinking, or better yet, provide a quotation from the person that shows what he or she was thinking?

When purchasing biographies for your library, give priority to books that fulfill curriculum needs. But you may also want biographies that are just wonderfully written and designed, about people the students may not know about (yet). Part of your job is to introduce students to these people, such as the first woman to swim the English Channel, in David Adler's *America's Champion Swimmer: Gertrude Ederle*, or G. F. Handel, joyfully celebrated in M. T. Anderson's *Handel: Who Knew What He Liked.* Don Brown has written several picture book biographies on figures probably unknown to kids, like moviemaker Mack Sennett. You will also want to find books that reflect a wide variety of subjects, not just "dead white guys" but also women, people of color, people from a variety of countries (not just the United States), and all types of careers, not just presidents or inventors. Include books on individuals who are still alive and people from the "pop culture" world: athletes, singers, actors, and other celebrities that students want to read about because this is "fun" reading. Of course the pop culture biographies should be as accurate, objective, well-designed, and documented as the other biographies on your shelves. Popular culture–related biographies generally work well when doing readers' advisory with reluctant readers.

Nonfiction for Young Children

Most nonfiction is written for children old enough to read, ages six and up. But there are a few nonfiction books and series that work well as read-alouds with preschoolers. Joanna Cole and Bruce Degan created the <u>Magic School Bus</u> books, which were adapted into an animated television series and are popular with a wide age range. The original books focused on science, but some of the more recent books explore history. The combination of humor, the magical teacher Ms. Frizzle, the cartoon dialogue balloons, and comical artwork works to make science fun and interesting to children.

Gail Gibbons writes and illustrates a wide variety of nonfiction picture books on animals, holidays, outer space, and nearly every topic of interest to three- to eight-year-olds. Her cartoon illustrations, usually done with bright colors and slim ink outlines, really look like picture book art. The text, usually a short paragraph under each full-page illustration, presents the facts in a simple, clear manner. Another solid nonfiction series for this age group, on science, is <u>Let's Read and Find Out</u> from HarperCollins. Many of these books were written by Franklyn M. Branley and can be read aloud to a preschooler. Several have been featured on PBS Television's *Reading Rainbow* series.

Often found in the picture book area, books by Byron Barton and Bob Barner are very colorfully illustrated informational books, not story books. Barton's factual books include *I Want to Be an Astronaut*, *Dinosaurs Dinosaurs*, and *Building a House*. Barner's simple nonfiction books include *Bugs! Bugs! Bugs!* and *Penguins, Penguins Everywhere*. Another author who writes simple factual books is Anne Rockwell. Hers are also likely to be found with the picture books, not with the Dewey numbered nonfiction, but they are factual. She often addresses topics of interest to preschoolers, like transportation, going to the doctor, and other common experiences for that age group. These three authors also write storybooks, but you can tell from the text if the book is factual or fictional.

Although not intended for children under the age of five, there are plenty of children's nonfiction books featuring dramatic photographs that interest preschoolers. Books in DK's <u>Eyewitness</u> series can be used by preschoolers who just want to look at the photographs of trains (or whatever the topic). Let young children check out these "coffee-table" style nonfiction books on topics they enjoy, like airplanes or dinosaurs or fire trucks, if they just want to look at the photos. "Reading" the pictures is an important step for the emergent reader.

Nonfiction for Recreational Reading

In conclusion, nonfiction offers a great alternative to novels when doing readers' advisory with 'tweens, many of whom prefer nonfiction or like a mix of novels and informational books. Younger children often enjoy nonfiction as well as picture books and easy readers, so they can look at the photographs. For some reluctant readers, only nonfiction is appealing. So when doing readers' advisory, remember to include nonfiction as well as fiction. After all, as adults we enjoy nonfiction, so why wouldn't children and 'tweens?

Helpful Books and Web Sites on Nonfiction for Children and 'Tweens

Following are some helpful reference books and Web sites on nonfiction for youth:

Barr, Catherine, and John T. Gillespie. *Best Books for Children: Preschool through Grade 6.* 9th ed. Westport, CT: Libraries Unlimited, 2010.

> Organized thematically, more than 25,000 books are described and recommended for children in this handy reference book. There is an entire section devoted to nonfiction.

Baxter, Kathleen A., and Marcia Agness Kochel. *Gotcha Good!: Nonfiction Books to Get Kids Excited About Reading.* Westport, CT: Libraries Unlimited, 2008.

> Baxter provides plenty of lists as well as booktalks on nonfiction books for children and 'tweens. Use the index to find lists of books on unusual but popular topics, such as monsters.

Candlewick's Ology Series. http://www.candlewick.com/ essentials.asp?browse=Title&mode=bkshlv&bkshlvi d=65&page=1&bkview=p&pix=y

> The Web site for Candlewick Publishers's Ology series, which includes *Oceanology, Spyology, Wizardology,* and other books with three-dimensional elements.

<u>Eyewitness</u> Books. http://us.dk.com/static/cs/us/11/features/eyewitness/

The Web site for the <u>Eyewitness</u> series of nonfiction books from Dorling Kindersley Publisher.

Sibert Award. http://www.ala.org/ala/mgrps/divs/alsc/awards grants/bookmedia/sibertmedal/index.cfm

The Web site for the Robert F. Sibert Informational Book Medal, given to nonfiction for youth by the Association of Library Service to Children, a division of the American Library Association.

NONFICTION FOR CHILDREN
AGES FIVE TO EIGHT

Aston, Dianna. *An Egg Is Quiet.*

Aston, Dianna. *A Seed Is Sleepy.*

Bishop, Nic. *Nic Bishop Frogs.*

Bishop, Nic. *Nic Bishop Spiders.*

Brewster, Hugh. *Dinosaurs in Your Backyard.*

Brown, Don. *All Stations! Distress! April 15, 1912, the Day the Titanic Sank.*

Butterworth, Chris. *Seahorse: The Shyest Fish in the Sea.*

Campbell, Sarah C. *Wolfsnail: A Backyard Predator.*

Dowson, Nick. *Tracks of a Panda.*

Fisher, Valorie. *How High Can a Dinosaur Count? And Other Math Mysteries.*

Frost, Helen. *Monarch and Milkweed.*

Goodman, Susan E. *All in Just One Cookie.*

Jenkins, Steve. *Actual Size.*

Jenkins, Steve. *Dogs and Cats.*

Jenkins, Steve. *How Many Ways Can You Catch a Fly?*

Jenkins, Steve. *Prehistoric Actual Size.*

Keller, Laurie. *Open Wide: Tooth School Inside.*

Kudlinki, Kathleen V. *Boy, Were We Wrong About the Solar System.*

Kuklin, Susan. *Families.*

Kurlansky, Mark. *The Story of Salt.*

Marrin, Albert. *Oh, Rats! The Story of Rats and People.*

Robbins, Ken. *Pumpkins.*

Schubert, Leda. *Ballet of the Elephants.*

Schwartz, David. *Where in the Wild? Camouflaged Creatures Concealed . . . and Revealed.*

Wheeler, Lisa. *Mammoths on the Move.*

NONFICTION FOR 'TWEENS

Anderson, Laurie Halse. *Independent Dames: What You Never Knew About the Women and Girls of the American Revolution.*

Arnosky, Jim. *Wild Tracks! A Guide to Nature's Footprints.*

Bartoletti, Susan Campbell. *Hitler Youth: Growing Up in Hitler's Shadow.*

Bartoletti, Susan Campbell. *Kids on Strike!*

Bausum, Ann. *Freedom Riders: John Lewis and Jim Zwerg on the Front Lines of the Civil Rights Movement.*

Bausum, Ann. *Muckrakers: How Ida Tarbell, Upton Sinclair, and Lincoln Steffers Helped Expose Scandal, Inspire Reform, and Invent Investigative Journalism.*

Burns, Loree Griffin. *Tracking Trash: Flotsam, Jetsam, and the Science of Ocean Motion.*

Coulter, Laurie. *When John & Caroline Lived in the White House.*

Deem, James M. *Bodies from the Ice: Melting Glaciers and the Recovery of the Past.*

Freedman, Russell. *Washington at Valley Forge.*

Giblin, James Cross. *The Many Rides of Paul Revere.*

Horne, Richard. *101 Things You Wish You Invented . . . and Some You Wish No One Had.*

Jackson, Donna M. *ER Vets: Life in an Animal Emergency Room.*

Macaulay, David. *The Way We Work: Getting to Know the Amazing Human Body.*

McPherson, James. *Fields of Fury: The American Civil War.*

Miles, Victoria. *Wild Science: Amazing Encounters Between Animals and the People Who Study Them.*

Murphy, Jim. *The American Plague: The True and Terrifying Story of the Yellow Fever Epidemic of 1793.*

National Children's Book and Literacy Alliance. *Our White House: Looking in, Looking Out.*

Nelson, Kadir. *We Are the Ship: The Story of Negro League Baseball.*

Patent, Dorothy Hinshaw. *When the Wolves Returned: Restoring Nature's Balance in Yellowstone.*

Pressler, Mirjam. *Anne Frank: A Hidden Life.*

Robbins, Ken. *Food for Thought: The Stories Behind the Things We Eat.*

Schlitz, Laura Amy. *Good Masters! Sweet Ladies! Voices from a Medieval Village.*

Scott, Elaine. *Mars and the Search for Life.*

Spitz, Bob. *Yeah! Yeah! Yeah! The Beatles, Beatlemania, and the Music That Changed the World.*

Thimmesh, Catherine. *Team Moon: How 400,000 People Landed Apollo 11 on the Moon.*

Various. <u>The Scientist in the Field</u> series.

Vogt, Robert. C. *Rain Forests.*

Wick, Walter. *A Drop of Water: A Book of Science and Wonder.*

BIOGRAPHIES FOR 'TWEENS

Bernier-Grand, Carmen T. *Cesar: Si Se Puede! Yes, We Can!*

Bernier-Grand, Carmen T. *Frida: Viva La Vida! Long Live Life!*

Bridges, Ruby. *Through My Eyes.*

Bryan, Ashley. *Words to My Life's Song.*

Fleischman, Sid. *Escape! The Story of the Great Houdini.*

Fleischman, Sid. *The Trouble Begins at Eight: A Life of Mark Twain in the Wild, Wild West.*

Fleming, Candace. *The Lincolns: A Scrapbook Look at Abraham and Mary.*

Freedman, Russell. *Babe Didrikson Zaharias: The Making of a Champion.*

Giblin, James Cross. *Good Brother, Bad Brother: The Story of Edwin Booth and John Wilkes Booth.*

Glover, Savion, and Bruce Weber. *Savion: My Life in Tap.*

Lawlor, Laurie. *Helen Keller: Rebellious Spirit.*

Maurer, Richard. *The Wright Sister: Katherine Wright and Her Famous Brothers.*

Partridge, Elizabeth. *John Lennon: All I Want Is the Truth.*

Partridge, Elizabeth. *This Land Was Made for You and Me: The Life and Songs of Woody Guthrie.*

Rosen, Michael. *Dickens: His Work and His World.*

Scieszka, Jon. *Knucklehead.*

Sis, Peter. *The Wall: Growing Up Behind the Iron Curtain.*

PICTURE BOOK BIOGRAPHIES

Aylesworth, Jim. *Our Abe Lincoln.*

Bardoe, Cheryl. *Gregor Mendel: The Friar Who Grew Peas.*

Grimes, Nikki. *Barack Obama: Son of Promise, Child of Hope.*

Kerley, Barbara. *Walt Whitman: Words for America.*

Kerley, Barbara. *What to Do About Alice? How Alice Roosevelt Broke the Rules, Charmed the World, and Drove Her Father Teddy Crazy!*

Nobleman, Marc Tyler. *Boys of Steel: The Creators of Superman.*

Rappaport, Doreen. *Abe's Honest Words: The Life of Abraham Lincoln.*

Rappaport, Doreen. *Eleanor, Quiet No More: The Life of Eleanor Roosevelt.*

Ray, Deborah Kogan. *Down the Colorado: John Wesley Powell, the One-Armed Explorer.*

Stone, Tanya Lee. *Elizabeth Leads the Way: Elizabeth Cady Stanton and the Right to Vote.*

Winter, Jonah. *Dizzy.*

Winter, Jonah. *Roberto Clemente: Pride of the Pittsburgh Pirates.*

Winter, Jonah, and Andy Carrilho. *You Never Heard of Sandy Koufax?!*

Yaccarino, Dan. *The Fantastic Undersea Life of Jacques Cousteau.*

POPULAR NONFICTION TOPICS

Pop-up and Toy Nonfiction for All Ages

Bolton, Anne. *Pyramids and Mummies.*

Gifford, Clive. *Robots.*

Gifford, Clive. *Spies Revealed.*

Manning, Mick. *Your Amazing Body.*

Platt, Richard, and David Hawcock. *Moon Landing: Apollo 11 40th Anniversary Pop-up.*

Putnam, James. *Egyptology.*

Sabuda, Robert. *Mega-beasts.*

Santoro, Lucio, and Meera Santoro. *Predators: A Pop-up Book with Revolutionary Technology.*

Steele, Philip. *A Knight's City.*

Steer, Dugard. *Dragonology.*

Steer, Dugard. *Pirateology.*

Steer, Dugard. *Wizardology.*

Gross Things for All Ages

Alton, Steve. *Blood and Goo and Boogers Too!*

Bennett, Bev. *Fear Factor Cookbook.*

Branzei, Sylvia. *Grossology.*

Branzei, Sylvia. *Grossology and You.*

Deem, James M. *Bodies from the Ice: Melting Glaciers and the Recovery of the Past.*

Fleischman, John. *Phineas Gage: A Gruesome but True Story About Brain Science.*

Goldish, Meish. *Spider-tizers and Other Creepy Treats.*

Sullivan, Robert. *Strange But True: The World's Weirdest Wonders.*

Walker, Sally M. *Written in Bone: Buried Lives of Jamestown and Colonial Maryland.*

From *Readers' Advisory for Children and 'Tweens* by Penny Peck.
Santa Barbara, CA: Libraries Unlimited. Copyright © 2010.

Chapter 9

Folklore for Children and 'Tweens

When a child or 'tween asks for a good book, we often go straight for fiction. We offer a picture book to read aloud as a bedtime story, beginning readers or easy chapter books to those learning how to read, and children's novels to 'tweens. How many times do you take them to the folk and fairy tales section? In many libraries folklore is shelved in Dewey 398.2, or in a section on its own, which makes it a few steps out of our reach and totally out of our thoughts. That is a shame, because folklore can be the perfect choice when a child asks for a great book to read, or for a parent who wants to read to the whole family.

Traditional Tales

Folk and fairy tales are sometimes referred to as traditional tales, and stem from an oral tradition. That's what makes them such great read-alouds for a family. These stories have magic, adventure, humor, and other qualities that are appealing to most readers and listeners. And even though folklore wasn't always for children, most of the books you find on the children's folklore shelves are suitable for all but the very youngest children. Of course a few might be too scary or too complex for young preschoolers, but many can be heartily recommended for the whole family.

Folklore: Great for Read-Alouds

Folklore was originally passed down orally by storytellers, not in written form. It includes myths, legends, and epic tales, as well as fables, folktales, fairy tales, and tall tales. For the most part, we don't know the original author of these traditional stories, but they are often attributed to the first person to record them, like Aesop, Mother Goose, Perrault, or the Brothers Grimm. These were not always considered "children's" stories, but rather stories for adults; some are very violent or sexual, and only in the past 150 years have they been deemed suitable for children. In the mid-1800s folktales were adapted to use with children, so they were "sanitized" of the more violent and sexual elements. Folklorists now generally frown on this practice and recommend that a folktale remain intact. Folktales have themes of good versus evil, lots of action and heroics, and other aspects that make them appealing to children.

Folklore also appeals to 'tweens; they appreciate the magical fantasy elements and the triumph of good over evil. Reluctant 'tween readers also enjoy folktales because the stories are usually shorter than a novel and often contain illustrations. Many teachers use folklore with the curriculum. For example, in middle school, when students study the Middle Ages, many teachers will read aloud a King Arthur tale.

The Importance of Source Notes

The best books containing traditional stories should above all retain the "storytelling" voice; these are stories meant to be read out loud. The books should also contain source notes, telling us from where the author obtained the story so we can verify its accuracy. Source notes can also help older 'tweens and adults find more books if they enjoy that one; they can look for the book cited as the original source of the story. If the 'tween is writing a report on the story, this may help him or her find other versions to compare or criticism to read.

Illustrations

If a tale is illustrated, the pictures should reflect the culture or country of origin accurately, as well as enhancing the story, not just be a showcase for the artist. The story should always come first. Individual folk and fairy tales are often published in picture book format, with rich, full-color illustrations and a paragraph of text that goes along with the artwork on each page, but the story should hold up on its own.

Princess Stories

Folk and fairy tales often come to mind when a child asks for certain types of books. For example, they can be good matches for those little girls asking for "princess books." Most libraries carry several different "Cinderella" stories from around the world. The child may have meant Disney princess stories, but after considering those, go to the fairy tales, too. Besides the commonly known European version of "Cinderella" by Charles Perrault, try some of these: *Little Gold Star: A Spanish American Cinderella Tale* by Robert D. San Souci, *Yeh-Shen: A Cinderella Story from China* by Ai-Ling Louie, *The Golden Sandal: A Middle Eastern Cinderella* by Rebecca Hickox, *The Gift of the Crocodile: A Cinderella Story* by Judy Sierra, or *The Gospel Cinderella* by Joyce Carol Thomas.

Scary Stories

Have you ever tried to find a book for a child or 'tween who is not an avid reader? When all your other recommendations fail, often these reluctant readers enjoy "scary" books. In addition to offering books like those in R. L. Stine's popular paperback series Goosebumps, try some of the wonderful scary folktale books. There are both collections of scary stories and a few individual illustrated tales that will please the young horror fan. Try some of these: *Scary Stories to Tell in the Dark* by Alvin Schwartz, and the sequels *More Scary Stories to Tell in the Dark* and *Scary Stories 3: More Tales to Chill Your Bones*; *Scared Witless: Thirteen Eerie Stories to Tell* by Martha Hamilton; *The Dark-Thirty: Southern Tales of the Supernatural* by Patricia McKissack; or *Short and Shivery: Thirty Chilling Tales* by Robert D. San Souci.

Folktales That Appeal to Boys

Folktales can also please young readers who want a short book. Many single illustrated folktales are perfect choices for children and 'tweens who are older than the picture book audience; they can be read in one sitting by 'tweens and hold their interest. Folktales also sometimes appeal to comic book fans or those who like action in their stories. Many tall tales fit this category, with dynamic characters like Paul Bunyan or John Henry. Give these a try: *Master Man* by Aaron Shepard, *The Elephant's Wrestling Match* by Judy Sierra, or *The Golem* by David Wisniewski.

Funny Folktale Spoofs

Readers of all ages enjoy humor, and your folklore section likely holds a wealth of "fractured fairy tales." Remember the fairy tale parodies on the *Rocky and Bullwinkle* television show? Many children's authors have created wonderfully funny fairy tale spoofs. These have special appeal to many 'tweens who like the still-popular *MAD* magazine (http://www.dccomics.com/mad/). Here are a few spoofs you can read to the whole family: *The Stinky Cheese Man and Other Fairly Stupid Tales* by Jon Scieszka, *The True Story of the Three Little Pigs* by Jon Scieszka, *Yo, Hungry Wolf* by David Vozar, or *Bigfoot Cinderrrrella* by Tony Johnston.

Fantasy Folklore

Fantasy has always been a popular genre with readers of all ages, and with the success of the <u>Harry Potter</u> books by J. K. Rowling, that popularity has skyrocketed. Many characters and motifs in current fantasy originated in folklore, including witches, magicians, fairies, dragons, unicorns, and other magical creatures. If a child or 'tween would like something with fantasy elements, offer some folklore along with the fantasy novels. In fact, consider doing a display that mixes fantasy with magical fairy tales. These titles have a wide age appeal: *Dragonology: The Complete Book of Dragons* by Dugald Steer (Candlewick, 2003); *Michael Hague's Magical World of Unicorns* by Michael Hague (Simon & Schuster, 1999); *King Arthur and the Round Table* by Hudson Talbott (Morrow, 1995); or *Young Merlin* by Robert D. San Souci (Doubleday, 1990). These often appeal to children and 'tweens who liked the *Lord of the Rings* and *Narnia* films.

Animal Tales

Many folktales feature animal characters that appeal to children who enjoy books such as E. B. White's *Charlotte's Web* or Kate DiCamillo's *Tale of Despereaux*. Aesop's fables are especially well suited to younger children because the stories are brief, and parents often request read-alouds that contain a message or "moral." There are both single illustrated tales and collections of animal tales and fables that can meet these requests. Give these a try: Margaret Read McDonald's *Mabela the Clever*, Rebecca Emberley's *Three Cool Kids*, and J. J. Reneaux's *How Animals Saved the People: Animal Tales from the South*.

Multicultural Folk and Fairy Tales

One aspect of folklore that appeals to us as educators is that the tales come from around the world, from all cultures that speak a language! So when you recommend folktales when doing readers' advisory, you are including stories from all over the world; the genre fully reflects the definition of multicultural. Consider including stories from many cultures that have a connection, demonstrating how some themes are universal; an often-used example is "Cinderella" (see "Princess Stories" above). There are at least twenty books in print featuring a Cinderella character from twenty different countries. But when looking for a folktale from any culture, be sure the book has a source note to explain the origin of the tale. Also, as mentioned above, the illustrations should honor the original culture from which the story came. Both Robert D. San Souci and Judy Sierra write folktale texts from various cultures around the world and are noted for their authentic adaptations that honor those cultures. They are often paired with illustrations that represent the culture of the tale, giving these adaptations even more authenticity.

Tales from African and African American Cultures

Several authors offer great African and African American folklore for children and families. Storyteller, author, and illustrator Ashley Bryan's books preserve that storytelling voice. Julius Lester has adapted several African American tall tales and Uncle Remus tales. Verna Aardema is not African American, but she has traveled to Africa several times and researches all of her adaptations. Jerry Pinkney has won several awards for writing and illustrating a variety of folktales.

Tales from Asian Cultures

Many folktales from the various countries in Asia have been adapted into picture books with rich illustrations. Demi has written and illustrated picture book–sized folktales from China and India. Ed Young has achieved dramatic retellings and award-winning illustrations for folktales, not just from China, where he was born, but also from Japan, India, and other parts of Asia.

Tales from Latino/Hispanic Cultures

There are not as many Latino folktales available for children as there are from other cultures. Hopefully the Pura Belpre Awards will help narrow that gap, because it has honored several authors and illustrators for their work adapting folktales, including Lulu Delacre, Pat Mora, Alma Flor Ada, and Joe Hayes.

Tales from European Cultures

Many authors and illustrators have adapted the Grimms' fairy tales, the tales by Perrault, and other European tales. Paul Galdone wrote and illustrated several popular folklore books that are perfect for young children and for use at storytime. James Marshall (who wrote the George and Martha picture books) has also adapted folktales and added his signature wit. For more elegant fairy tales, look at the work of Paul Zelinsky, whose adaptations of the Grimms' tales feature extensive source notes and are illustrated with Renaissance-like paintings. There are also many retellings of Charles Perrault's tales available.

Tales from Native American Cultures

Paul Goble has written and illustrated several award-winning folktales from Native American cultures. Born in England, he was honored by the Plains Indians and Chief Edgar Red Cloud for his authentic depictions of their culture. Joseph Bruchac is a noted Abenaki storyteller and author who has adapted folktales as well as written fiction for children. The Web site www.oyate.org also lists folklore.

Promoting Folk and Fairy Tales

For years libraries have hosted visiting, professional storytellers who expertly perform traditional tales from around the world. Many youth services librarians are trained to tell folktales from memory and to perform these stories at storytimes and other library programs. If you are hosting a storytelling program, promote the folktale collection with handouts of your favorite books or of newer folklore books in your collection. A book display can promote the upcoming program as well as market the books to the public before and after the event. Consider recording a podcast of a traditional tale or fable to put on your library's Web site.

Many fables and folktales have a moral or lesson, so offer them when parents ask for that type of material. Folklore truly has something for everyone. So next time you are helping a parent or teacher looking for read-aloud recommendations, or a child or 'tween who would like something scary, funny, short, and magical, don't overlook your folklore section. It contains treasures that will please even the pickiest reader.

Helfpul Books and Web Sites on Folklore for Youth

For more information on folk and fairy tales, try some of these resources:

American Folklore Society Aesop Award. http://www. afsnet.org/sections/children/

The American Folklore Society gives an annual award to the best children's folklore book. Check out the list of winners and honor books for ideas to suggest to families looking for read-alouds.

Bettelheim, Bruno. *The Uses of Enchantment: The Meaning and Importance of Fairy Tales.* New York: Penguin, 1991.

Bettelheim's work is the standard on the importance of traditional tales to a child's psychological well-being.

RECOMMENDED FOLKLORE/TRADITIONAL TALES FOR AGES FIVE TO TEN

Artell, Mike. *Petite Rouge: A Cajun Red Riding Hood.*

Balit, Christina. *Atlantis: The Legend of the Lost City.*

Brown, Marcia. *The Bun.*

Brown, Marcia. *Once a Mouse.*

Brown, Marcia. *Stone Soup.*

Carle, Eric. *The Rabbit and the Turtle: Aesop's Fables.*

Cohn, Amy L. *From Sea to Shining Sea: A Treasury of American Folklore and Folk Songs.*

Demi. *The Hungry Coat: A Tale from Turkey.*

Emberley, Rebecca. *Chicken Little.*

Emberley, Rebecca. *Three Cool Kids.*

Forest, Heather. *A Big Quiet House: A Yiddish Folktale from Eastern Europe.*

Galdone, Paul. Various folktales in picture book format.

Goldin, Barbara Diamond. *A Mountain of Blintzes.*

Gordon, Ruth. *Feathers.*

Harper, Wilhelmina. *The Gunniwolf.*

Hicks, Ray. *The Jack Tales.*

Huck, Charlotte. *The Black Bull of Norroway.*

Johnson-Davies, Denys. *Goha The Wise Fool.*

Kimmel, Eric. *Easy Work! An Old Tale.*

Lunge-Larsen, Lise. *The Troll with No Heart in His Body: And Other Tales of Trolls from Norway.*

Lynch, Tom. *Fables from Aesop.*

MacDonald, Margaret Read. *Fat Cat.*

MacDonald, Margaret Read. *Little Rooster's Diamond Button.*

MacDonald, Margaret Read. *Tunjur! Tunjur! Tunjur!*

Martin, Rafe. *The Brave Little Parrot.*

Martin, Rafe. *The Shark God.*

Mayer, Marianna. *Women Warriors: Myths and Legends of Heroic Women.*

Mayes, Walter. *Walter the Giant Storyteller's Giant Book of Giant Stories.*

Oberman, Sheldon. *Solomon and the Ant and Other Jewish Folktales.*

Osborne, Mary Pope. *American Tall Tales.*

Osborne, Mary Pope. *New York's Bravest.*

Prose, Francine. *The Demon's Mistake.*

Prose, Francine. *You Never Know: The Legend of the Lamed-Vavniks.*

Pullman, Philip. *Puss in Boots.*

Reneaux, J. J. *How Animals Saved the People: Animal Tales from the South.*

Salley, Coleen. *Who's That Tripping Over My Bridge?*

San Souci, Robert. *Brave Margaret.*

San Souci, Robert. *Cut from the Same Cloth: American Women of Myth, Legend, and Tall Tale.*

Sanfield, Steve. *Strudel, Strudel, Strudel.*

Sierra, Judy. *Beautiful Butterfly.*

Ward, Helen. *Rooster and the Fox.*

Willey, Margaret. *Clever Beatrice.*

Wolkstein, Diane. *Sun Mother Wakes the World: An Australian Creation Story.*

Zelinsky, Paul O. *Rapunzel.*

Zelinsky, Paul O. *Rumplestiltskin.*

Zeman, Ludmila. *Sindbad: From the Tales of the Thousand and One Nights.*

PRINCESS FOLKTALES FOR
AGES FIVE TO TEN

Climo, Shirley. *The Irish Cinderlad.*

Climo, Shirley. *The Korean Cinderella.*

Climo, Shirley. *The Persian Cinderella.*

Coburn, Jewell Reinhart. *Angkat: The Cambodian Cinderella.*

Coburn, Jewell Reinhart. *Jouanah: A Hmong Cinderella.*

Dalton, Annie. *The Starlight Princess and Other Princess Stories.*

Daly, Jude. *Fair, Brown, and Trembling: An Irish Cinderella Story.*

De La Paz, Myrna J. *Abadeha: The Philippine Cinderella.*

DePaola, Tomie. *Adelita: A Mexican Cinderella Story.*

Fleischman, Paul. *Glass Slipper, Gold Sandal: A Worldwide Cinderella.*

Hickox, Rebecca. *The Golden Sandal: A Middle Eastern Cinderella Story.*

Isadora, Rachel. *The Twelve Dancing Princesses.*

Jaffe, Nina. *The Way Meat Loves Salt: A Cinderella Tale from the Jewish Tradition.*

Louie, Ai-Ling. *Yeh-Shen: A Cinderella Story from China.*

Martin, Rafe. *The Rough-Face Girl.*

Mehta, Lila. *Anklet for a Princess: A Cinderella Story from India.*

Perrault, Charles. *Cinderella.*

Pollock, Penny. *The Turkey Girl: A Zuni Cinderella.*

San Souci, Robert. *Little Gold Star: A Spanish American Cinderella Tale.*

San Souci, Robert. *Sootface: An Ojibwa Cinderella Story.*

Sierra, Judy. *The Gift of the Crocodile: A Cinderella Story.*

Steptoe, John. *Mufaro's Beautiful Daughters: An African Tale.*

Thomas, Joyce Carol. *The Gospel Cinderella.*

SCARY FOLKTALES FOR AGES
SEVEN TO TWELVE

Goode, Diane. *Diane Goode's Book of Scary Stories and Songs.*

Hague, Michael. *Kate Culhane: A Ghost Story.*

Hamilton, Martha, and Mitch Weiss. *Scared Witless: Thirteen Eerie Tales to Tell.*

Haskins, Jim. *The Headless Haunt and Other African-American Ghost Stories.*

Haskins, Jim. *Moaning Bones: African-American Ghost Stories.*

Hurston, Nora Zeale. *The Skull Talks Back and Other Haunting Tales.*

Kimmel, Eric. *Gershon's Monster: A Story for the Jewish New Year.*

Lyons, Mary E. *Raw Head and Bloody Bones: African-American Tales of the Supernatural.*

McKissack, Patricia. *The Dark Thirty: Southern Tales of the Supernatural.*

Medearis, Angela Shelf. *Tailypo: A Newfangled Tall Tale.*

San Souci, Robert. *The Hobyahs.*

San Souci, Robert. Short and Shivery series.

Schwartz, Alvin. Scary Stories to Tell in the Dark series.

Wisniewski, David. *The Golem.*

MULTICULTURAL FOLKTALES FOR AGES SIX TO TEN

African and African American

Aardema, Verna. *Misoso.*

Aardema, Verna. *Why Mosquitoes Buzz in People's Ears.*

Badoe, Adwoa. *The Pot of Wisdom: Ananse Stories.*

Bryan, Ashley. *Beautiful Blackbird.*

Cummings, Pat. *Ananse and the Lizard.*

Daly, Niki. *Pretty Salma: A Little Red Riding Hood Story from Africa.*

Diakite, Baba Wague. *The Hatseller and the Monkeys.*

Diakite, Baba Wague. *The Hunterman and the Crocodile.*

Gershator, Phillis. *Only One Cowry: A Dahomean Tale.*

Haley, Gail E. *A Story, a Story.*

Hamilton, Virginia. *Bruh Rabbit and the Tar Baby Girl.*

Hamilton, Virginia. *The Girl Who Spun Gold*

Hamilton, Virginia. *The People Could Fly.*

Hurston, Zora Neale. *What's the Hurry, Fox? And Other Animal Stories.*

Lester, Julius. *John Henry.*

Lester, Julius. *Tales of Uncle Remus.*

MacDonald, Margaret Read. *Mabela the Clever.*

McDermott, Gerald. *Anansi the Spider: A Tale from the Ashanti.*

McDermott, Gerald. *The Magic Tree: A Tale from the Congo.*

McKissack, Patricia. *Tales of Slicksters, Tricksters, and Other Wily Characters.*

Pinkney, Jerry. *Little Red Riding Hood.*

Shepard, Aaron. *Master Man.*

Sierra, Judy. *The Elephant's Wrestling Match.*

Tchana, Katrin. *Sense Pass King: A Story from Cameroon.*

Wolkstein, Diane. *The Day the Ocean Came to Visit.*

Asian Cultures

Berger, Barbara Helen. *All the Way to Lhasa.*

Casanova, Mary. *The Hunter.*

Compestine, Ying Chang. *The Real Stone Soup.*

Demi. *The Donkey and the Rock.*

Eimon, Mina Harada. *Why Cats Chase Mice: A Story of the Twelve Zodiac Signs.*

Han, Suzanne Crowder. *The Rabbit's Escape.*

Han, Suzanne Crowder. *The Rabbit's Judgment.*

Han, Suzanne Crowder. *The Rabbit's Tale.*

Hodges, Margaret. *The Boy Who Drew Cats.*

Hong, Chen Jiang. *The Magic Horse of Han Gan.*

Hong, Lily Toy. *Two of Everything.*

Jaffe, Nina. *Older Brother, Younger Brother: A Korean Folktale.*

Kimmel, Eric. *The Rooster's Antlers: A Story of the Chinese Zodiac.*

Kimmel, Eric. *Ten Suns: A Chinese Legend.*

Kimmel, Eric. *Three Samurai Cats: A Story from Japan.*

MacDonald, Margaret Read. *Go to Sleep, Gecko! A Balinese Folktale.*

Morimoto, Junko. *Two Bullies.*

Muth, Jon. *Stone Soup.*

Poole, Amy Lowry. *The Ant and the Grasshopper.*

Poole, Amy Lowry. *How the Rooster Got His Crown.*

San Souci, Robert. *Pedro and the Monkey.*

Sellier, Marie. *What the Rat Told Me: A Legend of the Chinese Zodiac.*

Sierra, Judy. *Tasty Baby Belly Buttons.*

Young, Ed. *I, Doko: The Tale of a Basket.*

Young, Ed. *The Sons of the Dragon King: A Chinese Legend.*

Young, Ed. *What About Me?*

Latino/Hispanic

Alvarez, Julia. *A Gift of Gracias.*

Alvarez, Julia. *The Secret Footprints.*

Campoy, F. Isabel, and Alma Flor Ada. *Tales Our Abuelitas Told.*

Deedy, Carmen Agra. *Martina the Beautiful Cockroach: A Cuban Folktale.*

Delacre, Lulu. *Golden Tales: Myths, Legends, and Folktales from Latin America.*

Gerson, Mary-Joan. *Fiesta Femenina: Celebrating Women in Mexican Folktale.*

Gerson, Mary-Joan. *How Night Came from the Sea: A Story From Brazil.*

Hayes, Joe. *Juan Verdades: The Man Who Couldn't Tell a Lie.*

Kimmel, Eric. *The Two Mountains: An Aztec Legend.*

McDermott, Gerald. *Jabuti the Tortoise: A Trickster Tale from the Amazon.*

Montes, Marisa. *Juan Bobo Goes to Work: A Puerto Rican Folktale.*

Mora, Pat. *The Race of Toad and Deer.*

Morales, Yuyi. *Just a Minute: A Trickster Tale and Counting Book.*

Philip, Neil. *Horse Hooves and Chicken Feet: Mexican Folktales.*

Native American

Ata, Te. *Baby Rattlesnake.*

Bierhorst, John. *Is My Friend at Home?*

Bierhorst, John. *The Woman Who Fell from the Sky.*

Bruchac, Joseph. *How Chipmunk Got His Stripes.*

Bruchac, Joseph. *Turtle's Race with Beaver.*

Erdrich, Louise. *Bears Make Rock Soup.*

Goble, Paul. *Girl Who Loved Wild Horses.*

Goble, Paul. *Her Seven Brothers.*

Goble, Paul. <u>Iktomi</u> series.

Goble, Paul. *Star Boy.*

Goble, Paul. *Storm Maker's Tipi.*

Hall, Amanda. *The Stolen Sun: A Story of Native Alaska.*

Heller, Janet Ruth. *How the Moon Regained Her Shape.*

Lelooska, Chief. *Spirit of the Cedar People.*

London, Jonathan. *Fire Race: A Karak Coyote Tale.*

McDermott, Gerald. *Raven: A Trickster Tale from the Pacific Northwest.*

Norman, Howard. *Trickster and the Fainting Birds.*

Philip, Neil. *The Great Mystery: Myths of Native America.*

Rosen, Michael. *The Dog Who Walked with God.*

Ross, Gayle. *How Rabbit Tricked Otter and Other Cherokee Trickster Stories.*

San Souci, Robert. *Two Bear Cubs.*

Chapter 10

Poetry for Children and 'Tweens

During readers' advisory sessions, children or 'tweens sometimes request "a short book," "a book with cartoon drawings," or "a funny book." These are all characteristics you can find in books on poetry shelves, but how often do you go to the poetry section when helping a child find recreational reading? Poetry can be a great choice for many children, especially reluctant readers who find novels too long or too demanding. A poetry collection can be just as satisfying as a novel, yet not be as intimidating to some students who are still struggling with reading skills.

Some 'tweens may be reluctant to try poetry, if they have had English classes in which poems were analyzed. At first glance, poetry reading may sound too much like homework. Show these 'tweens Shel Silverstein's books or other popular poetry collections; they may be more open-minded once they realize you are not going to ask them about metaphor or symbolism. In fact, younger children are often delighted with poetry; their first books are Mother Goose or Dr. Seuss rhyming stories. A few 'tweens will return to that interest in poetry when offered many of the delightful books in your collection, and when they realize they don't have to write a term paper about the poems.

Single Illustrated Poems for Picture Book Fans

Many poems are published in a picture book format, even though they may be better suited to a child in school, and not a preschooler. Look for single poems that are served by the illustrations, not ones that are the vehicle for an artist. Also, avoid abridged or adapted poems, and look for those for which the original source is cited. Some great examples are *Black Cat* by Christopher Myers; Ntozake Shange's *Ellington Was Not a Street*; Ernest Thayer's *Casey at the Bat*, with illustrations by Christopher Bing; and Longfellow's *Paul Revere's Ride*, with illustrations by Ted Rand.

Humorous Poetry Collections for a Wide Age Range

Humorous poetry collections are clearly the most popular types of poetry books for children and 'tweens; just look for Shel Silverstein's name on the best-seller lists. There are many great poetry collections that contain funny poems by one author, enhanced by cartoon-style illustrations that enhance the poetry. Silverstein illustrated his own books, but Jack Prelutsky is nearly as popular, and many of his books were illustrated by James Stevenson. These can be a boon to reluctant readers, because they are as thick as "real" books for 'tweens but are easier to read because the cartoons help the reader decode the text. If a child or 'tween asks for "a funny book, but not too long," these often fill the bill. These are some of the most popular humorous poetry collections: *Where the Sidewalk Ends* by Shel Silverstein, *My Dog May Be a Genius* by Jack Prelutsky, *Antarctic Antics: A Book of Penguin Poems* by Judy Sierra, and *Timothy Tunny Swallowed a Bunny* by Bill Grossman.

Poetry for 'Tween Sports Fans

As discussed in chapter 6, not as many sports novels are being published as in the past. But several attractive and interesting poetry collections celebrate sports, and you can offer these as reading options. If a child or 'tween doesn't seem interested in any books, and says his or her hobby is a sport, consider these titles: *Rimshots: Basketball Pix, Rolls, and Rhythms* by Charles R. Smith; *For the Love of the Game: Michael Jordan and Me* by Eloise Greenfield; and *Sports Pages* by Arnold Adoff.

Multicultural Poetry for a Wide Age Range

Multicultural poetry has been popular with children since *Bronzeville Boys and Girls* by Gwendolyn Brooks was first published in 1956. There are collections from many cultures that speak to children, with evocative poems paired with dramatic illustrations. Be sure to include multicultural poetry collections when a teacher, parent, or child asks for books celebrating a certain culture. Here are some favorites: *My Chinatown* by Kam Mak, *A Movie in My Pillow* by Jorge Argueta, *Neighborhood Odes* by Gary Soto, *Gingerbread Days* by Joyce Carol Thomas, and *A Pocketful of Poems* by Nikki Grimes.

Poetry Collections for Family Read-Alouds

When choosing poetry anthologies for a 'tween or a family, look for collections that offer more than just the same old poems found in many collections, including textbooks. Look for collections that mix old and new poems. If a poem is adapted or abridged, make sure that fact is indicated clearly; better yet, try to find collections that do not shorten poems but offer the entire work as the author intended. It is helpful when a collection cites the source for each poem, too, so you can find the original source if you want. Illustrations should suit the poems and not crowd the page. Poems are meant to be set on pages with plenty of white space to allow the reader to pause as the author intended. See the poetry anthologies listed at the end of this chapter.

Novels in Poetry Form

Many reluctant readers find novels too daunting; the amount of text simply overwhelms some 'tweens. But there are several high-quality novels written in free verse that appeal to a wide range of readers, while still giving 'tweens literature of substance. The Newbery Medal winner *Out of the Dust* by Karen Hesse is a novel in free verse that has a quiet dignity, evoking the Great Depression in the United States. Because it is in a free verse format, many 'tweens who are hesitant to read a long novel will pick it up. Other novels in free verse followed Hesse's success; these can be great to recommend to 'tweens who want a "good book for a book report," but don't want something too long. See the list at the end of the chapter for some novels written in free verse that have proven popular with 'tweens.

Promoting Poetry as Recreational Reading

You can promote your poetry collection through the usual displays and handouts, as well as special poetry programs. April is National Poetry Month, which offers a great opportunity for programming. Have a poetry-writing contest and post the winners to the library's Web site. Have a poetry "slam" for 'tweens and teens, complete with a coffeehouse atmosphere and refreshments. Host a favorite poet at your library; if no one is close or affordable enough to come to the library, do a virtual visit over the Internet using Skype or other technology whereby you can hear and see the author on the computer screen.

Of course poetry can be promoted all year long, not just in April. You can promote a new poet every month, perhaps in celebration of the poet's birthday. For example, Jack Prelutsky's birthday is in September; make a simple display of his books with a photo of the author. His books will be picked up because of their engaging cartoon covers. Also, be sure to include poetry books in other displays. If you are doing an Earth Day theme, with books about recycling or the environment, include a few poetry books on that subject. If you are doing a Halloween display, there are plenty of related poetry books, such as scary poetry anthologies, including Poe's "The Raven," and funny monster poetry collections such as Adam Rex's *Frankenstein Makes a Sandwich.*

Poetry appeals to a wide array of readers, from reluctant readers to the angst-filled middle schooler who loves Emily Dickinson, to 'tweens who like to write poetry. Poetry can be an unexpected surprise to the student who asks for help finding a good book to read. At the end of the readers' advisory exchange, the reader may take some of the novels you suggested along with the poetry books you showed. Poetry can also be a nice "dessert" offering after you have showed the 'tween the "main entree" of genre fiction, and many young people will read and enjoy poetry even if they won't finish some of the longer novels you've suggested.

Helpful Books and Web Sites on Poetry for Youth

For those interested in promoting poetry, Lee Bennett Hopkins's book is an essential tool, filled with a variety of programming ideas as well as short biographies of several poets. There are also several Web sites featuring poetry in the public domain, and poet's Web sites, but none is quite as useful as Hopkins's book.

Hopkins, Lee Bennett. *Pass the Poetry, Please!* 3rd ed. New York: HarperCollins, 1998.

Hopkins's enthusiasm for promoting poetry to children is contagious, and this guide is filled with ideas for promoting poetry without analyzing or dissecting it in a way that turns 'tweens off.

Shel Silverstein. http://www.shelsilverstein.com/indexSite. html

Silverstein's Web site is filled with fun things for kids to do and has an area for teachers and librarians with ideas on using his poetry with children.

RECOMMENDED POETRY BOOKS FOR AGES SEVEN TO TWELVE

Bulion, Leslie. *Hey There, Stink Bug!*

Fleischman, Paul. *Joyful Noise: Poems for Two Voices.*

Florian, Douglas. *Bow Wow Meow Meow.*

Florian, Douglas. *Comets, Stars, the Moon, and Mars.*

Florian, Douglas. *Dinothesaurus.*

Franco, Betsy. *Mathematickles.*

Janeczko, Paul. *A Kick in the Head: An Everyday Guide to Poetic Forms.*

Katz, Alan. *Going, Going, Gone! And Other Silly Dilly Sports Songs.*

Kennedy, Caroline. *A Family of Poems: My Favorite Poetry for Children.*

Kennedy, X. J., and Dorothy M. Kennedy. *Knock at a Star: A Child's Introduction to Poetry, Revised Edition.*

Marsalis, Wynton. *Jazz ABZ: An A to Z Collection of Jazz Portraits.*

Martin, Bill, Jr., ed. *The Bill Martin, Jr. Big Book of Poetry.*

Milne, A. A. *House at Pooh Corner.*

Milne, A. A. *Now We Are Six.*

Prelutsky, Jack. *Good Sports: Rhymes about Running, Jumping, Throwing, and More.*

Prelutsky, Jack. *The Swamps of Sleethe: Poems Beyond the Solar System.*

Rex, Adam. *Frankenstein Makes a Sandwich.*

Scieszka, Jon. *Science Verse.*

Sidman, Joyce. *Butterfly Eyes and Other Secrets of the Meadow.*

Sidman, Joyce. *Song of the Water Boatman and Other Pond Poems.*

Stevenson, James. <u>Corn</u> series.

Stevenson, James. *Just Around the Corner: Poems.*

Stevenson, Robert Louis. *A Child's Garden of Verses.*

Wilson, Karma. *What's the Weather Inside?*

Worth, Valerie. <u>Small Poems</u> series.

MULTICULTURAL POETRY FOR AGES SEVEN TO TWELVE

African American Poetry

Bryan, Ashley. *Ashley Bryan's ABC of African American Poetry.*

Feelings, Tom. *Soul Looks Back in Wonder.*

Giovanni, Nikki. *Spin a Soft Black Song.*

Greenfield, Eloise. *For the Love of the Game: Michael Jordan and Me.*

Greenfield, Eloise. *Night on Neighborhood Street.*

Grimes, Nikki. *Pocketful of Poems.*

Hughes, Langston. *Langston Hughes: Poetry for Young People.*

Medina, Tony. *DeShawn Days.*

Myers, Walter Dean. *Blues Journey.*

Shange, Ntozake. *Ellington Was Not a Street.*

Shore, Diane Z., and Jessica Alexander. *This Is the Dream.*

Thomas, Joyce Carol. *The Blacker the Berry.*

Thomas, Joyce Carol. *Brown Honey and Broom Wheat Tea.*

Thomas, Joyce Carol. *Gingerbread Days.*

Asian American Poetry

Gollub, Matthew. *Cool Melons Turn to Frogs: The Life and Poems of Issa.*

Kobayashi, Issa. *Today and Today.*

Mak, Kam. *My Chinatown: One Year in Poems.*

Park, Linda Sue. *Tap Dancing on the Roof.*

Various. *Maples in the Mist: Children's Poems from the Tang Dynasty.*

Wong, Janet S. *A Suitcase Full of Seaweed, and Other Poems.*

Young, Ed. *Beyond the Great Mountains: A Visual Poem about China.*

Latino/Hispanic Poetry

Alarcon, Francisco X. *Angels Ride Bikes and Other Fall Poems.*

Alarcon, Francisco X. *From the Bellybutton of the Moon and Other Summer Poems.*

Alarcon, Francisco X. *Iguanas in the Snow and Other Winter Poems.*

Alarcon, Francisco X. *Laughing Tomatoes and Other Spring Poems.*

Argueta, Jorge. *A Movie in My Pillow.*

Carlson, Lori M. *Sol a Sol: Bilingual Poems.*

Mora, Pat. *Confetti: Poems for Children.*

Mora, Pat. *Love to Mama: A Tribute to Mothers.*

Mora, Pat. *Yum! Mmmm! Que Rico! Americas' Sproutings.*

Soto, Gary. *Neighborhood Odes.*

Native American Poetry

Philip, Neil. *Weave Little Stars into My Sleep.*

Sneve, Virginia Driving Hawk. *Dancing Teepees: Poems of American Indian Youth.*

Various. *When the Rain Sings: Poems by Young Native Americans.*

HUMOROUS POETRY FOR ALL AGES

Dahl, Roald. *Vile Verses.*

Grossman, Bill. *Timothy Tunny Swallowed a Bunny.*

Katz, Alan. *Oops!*

Moss, Jeff. *The Butterfly Jar.*

Numeroff, Laura. *Sometimes I Wonder If Poodles Like Noodles.*

Prelutsky, Jack. *My Dog May Be a Genius: Poems.*

Prelutsky, Jack. *The New Kid on the Block: Poems.*

Prelutsky, Jack. *Something Big Has Been Here.*

Sierra, Judy. *Antarctic Antics: A Book of Penguin Poems.*

Silverstein, Shel. *A Light in the Attic.*

Silverstein, Shel. *Where the Sidewalk Ends.*

POETRY ANTHOLOGIES FOR ALL AGES

Brown, Marc. *Scared Silly! A Book for the Brave.*

Bryan, Ashley. *ABC of African-American Poetry.*

Clinton, Catherine. *I, Too, Sing America: Three Centuries of African-American Poetry.*

Clinton, Catherine. *A Poem of Her Own: Voices of American Women Yesterday and Today.*

DePaola, Tomie. *Tomie DePaola's Book of Poems.*

Hollyer, Belinda. *She's All That! Poems About Girls.*

Hopkins, Lee Bennett. *Climb into My Lap: First Poems to Read Together.*

Hopkins, Lee Bennett. *My America: A Poetry Atlas of the United States.*

Hopkins, Lee Bennett. *Side by Side: Poems to Read Together.*

James, Simon. *Days Like This.*

Janeczko, Paul. *A Kick in the Head.*

Janeczko, Paul. *A Poke in the I: A Collection of Concrete Poems.*

Nicholls, Judith. *Someone I Like: Poems About People.*

Prelutsky, Jack. *The Beauty of the Beast.*

Prelutsky, Jack. *The Random House Book of Poetry for Children.*

Prelutsky, Jack. *The 20th Century Children's Poetry Collection.*

Schwartz, Alvin. *And the Green Grass Grows All Around: Folk Poetry for Everyone.*

Steptoe, Javaka. *In Daddy's Arms I Am Tall: African Americans Celebrating Fathers.*

Various. *Sing a Song of Popcorn: Every Child's Book of Poems.*

Whipple, Laura. *Celebrating America.*

Yolen, Jane. *Here's A Little Poem: A Very First Book of Poetry.*

NOVELS IN FREE VERSE FOR AGES NINE TO TWELVE

Brown, Susan Taylor. *Hugging the Rock.*

Bryant, Jennifer. *Ringside, 1925: Views from the Scopes Trial.*

Bryant, Jennifer. *The Trial.*

Carvell, Marlene. *Sweetgrass Basket.*

Cormier, Robert. *Frenchtown Summer.*

Creech, Sharon. *Hate That Cat.*

Creech, Sharon. *Love That Dog.*

Darrow, Sharon. *Trash.*

Grimes, Nikki. *Dark Sons.*

Hesse, Karen. *Out of the Dust.*

Hesse, Karen. *Witness.*

Roy, Jennifer. *Yellow Star.*

Smith, Hope Anita. *Keeping the Night Watch.*

Smith, Hope Anita. *The Way a Door Closes.*

Spinelli, Eileen. *Summerhouse Time.*

Spinelli, Eileen. *Where I Live.*

Williams, Vera. *Amber Was Brave, Essie Was Smart.*

Woodson, Jacqueline. *Locomotion.*

Zimmer, Tracie Vaughn. *Reaching for Sun.*

Chapter 11

Graphic Novels and Magazines

When many longtime librarians think of graphic novels, we think "young adult." When graphic novels first came into libraries, most seemed age appropriate for YA (ages twelve and up), rather than for a younger audience. But that is rapidly changing; there are now graphic novel series that appeal to children, like <u>Babymouse</u> by Jennifer Holm and Matthew Holm. However, graphic novels are still generally shelved in the young adult area of many libraries. Graphic novels also appeal to many 'tweens, both those who love reading and reluctant readers. That's one of the great aspects of graphic novels—they might appeal to a person who reads long, involved novels just as much as they appeal to a 'tween who would never read a novel for pleasure.

Characteristics of Graphic Novels

One way to describe graphic novels is to think of them as literary comic books. The stories are often thoughtful, and the artwork helps to tell the story along with the text. Before Art Spiegelman's <u>Maus</u> series (an allegory about the Holocaust), many people saw this format as glorified comic books, but when <u>Maus</u> won the Pulitzer Prize, that attitude began to change. Frank Miller's <u>Dark Knight</u> series, featuring Batman, also helped to change opinions of this format. Now it is a given that most middle and high school libraries and public libraries will carry a wide variety of graphic novels for 'tweens.

Graphic novels appeal to many different age groups, depending on the length of the story, the subject matter, and the grade level of the text. So there are graphic novels for both children and 'tweens, and they can fall into several different genres, from humorous stories to horror. Some graphic novels are listed at the end of this chapter, divided by grade level.

A good tool to help you learn about graphic novels is the Web site No Flying, No Tights (www.noflyingnotights.com). Notice that the site is divided into three areas: "Sidekicks," which covers graphic novels for children; the main area, which details graphic novels for teens; and "The Lair," which is the newest area, devoted to graphic novels for older teens and adults (ages sixteen and up). Some graphic novels, like Jeff Smith's Bone series, appeal to a wide age range.

Graphic novels have become essential in the library collection; they are popular with boys (as well as girls), encourage those who don't enjoy novels to continue reading, and convince those readers that they can find value in the library. Graphic novels may even be the bridge to longer, more text-heavy books. If you are building your library's graphic novel section for children and 'tweens, be sure to look at the "Sidekicks" area of www.noflyingnotights.com.

Because graphic novels contain such a wide variety of themes and plotlines, not all are suited to children. Some are only appropriate for older teens and adults due to the violence and sexuality in both the text and illustrations. Even though they may look like comic books, not all graphic novels are easy to read. Some are very complex, as well as dealing with intense subjects, so be sure to know the content of any graphic novel you recommend to a child or 'tween. Read as many as possible in your collection, or at least try to thumb through them to get a feel for the content. Also, read the reviews of the graphic novels in your collection; they can help you pinpoint the appropriate grade or age level for that title.

Award-Winning Graphic Novels

Two graphic novels for 'tweens have won awards, which makes it easier for school librarians to justify purchasing this format. *Pedro and Me* was named a Sibert Honor book (the award given by ALA/ALSC for best nonfiction for children up to age fourteen). It was the first graphic novel to win a children's book award, although most of us would probably consider *Pedro and Me* as suitable for ages twelve and up. It is the true story of AIDS activist Pedro Zamora, who was on the third season of

MTV's *The Real World*, and was written by fellow cast member and cartoonist Judd Winick. The other award-winning graphic novel is *American Born Chinese* by Gene Yang, which won the Printz Award for best young adult book in 2007. The fact that these two books won awards not intended for graphic novels, but for "literature," really gives the format a gravitas. *American Born Chinese* is suitable for older 'tweens (ages ten and up).

Manga

Manga is graphic novels done in the style of Japanese animated films (anime), with big-eyed characters and boys who are almost feminine in facial features. <u>Nancy Drew</u> and the <u>Hardy Boys</u> have been adapted into the graphic novel format, with manga-style artwork. Other manga series that are popular with 'tweens include <u>Dragonball Z</u>, <u>Pokemon</u>, and some from the publisher Paper Cutz (www.papercutz. com/).

The publisher Scholastic recently started a subdivision just for graphic novels, Graphix (www.scholastic.com/graphix/), which publishes many graphic novels aimed at 'tweens, such as Jeff Smith's <u>Bone</u> series, a graphic version of Ann Martin's *Babysitter Club*, and *The Stonekeeper* by Kazu Kibuishi.

Another great source for quality graphic novels is the Center for Cartoon Studies, which has published a few with Hyperion. I have read three, all nonfiction/biographical graphic novels, on Harry Houdini, Satchel Paige, and Henry David Thoreau. Visit www.cartoonstudies.org for more information.

Magazines

When doing readers' advisory, how often do you think of magazines? In some instances magazines are the best match for the topic requested by 'tweens. As in graphic novels, photos and illustrations are important. Also like some graphic novels, magazines come out monthly or bimonthly. Magazines often appeal to very reluctant readers, who like to flip through and look at the pictures. Certain topics, like popular sports, music, and movie stars, are featured in some teen magazines but may not be in books in the biography section.

When you think of magazines for kids, what comes to mind? For me, it's reading *Jack and Jill* or *Highlights* at the dentist's office. These two classics are still found in libraries and are still read by kids. Tom Hanks mentioned *My Weekly Reader* in one of his Oscar speeches, and this school staple is still going strong after 100 years! Newer magazines, such as *Sports Illustrated for Kids* and *J-14*, are also well thumbed, but many young readers are depending more on Web sites for browsing reading than on magazines. If a 'tween likes to read on the computer but won't read a book, maybe he or she will read a magazine. 'Tweens often read magazines in the online version, so when it is time to check out reading material, they may take a magazine if you show them where they are located.

Which Magazines Are Popular?

Why do libraries carry magazines for kids, and which ones do they carry? For the most part, magazines for children and 'tweens are for recreational reading, not so much for research; this appears to be the case in school libraries as well as public libraries. The magazines that seem to be popular include *J-14*, *Boys Life*, *Girls Life*, *American Girl*, anything to do with video games, and *MAD Magazine*, which gets "worn out" at my library. There are some newer magazines, like *New Moon*, which is about girl empowerment, and the line of literary magazines from Cricket, which publishes writing by children. The Cricket line includes *Baby Bug*, *Ladybug*, *Spider*, and *Cicada* (for teens). There is also *Cobblestone*, a history magazine for kids; *Muse*, which is like a museum in a magazine; *Odyssey* (about astronomy); and several related to popular culture, such as *Sports Illustrated for Kids*. *Nickelodeon*, *Nick Jr.*, and *Disney Adventures* used to be popular, but they stopped publication.

If the 'tween has expressed an interest in music or movie stars during the readers' advisory interview, he or she might enjoy the magazines *J-14*, *Twist*, or *Popstar*. These all feature photos and articles on actors, singers, and other popular culture idols. *Right on!* magazine focuses on African American pop culture figures.

If the 'tween likes sports stars,, try *Sports Illustrated for Kids* or *Transworld Skateboarding*. *Thrasher* is another popular skateboarding magazine, but many libraries only recommend this to older teens because some of the advertising is not appropriate for 'tweens. *WWE* is a very popular wrestling magazine with 'tweens; middle schoolers can enjoy it, but the scantily clad lady wrestlers may not be suitable for children or for an elementary school library.

For those who enjoy video games, there are several popular gaming magazines. *Nintendo Power*, *PC Gamer*, and *Gamepro* are all in demand by the same 'tweens who come to your gaming programs. Readers are often looking for cheat codes, which are published in these and other video game magazines.

Fashion magazines for 'tweens are also popular. *Seventeen* magazine has been popular for generations. In a similar mode is *Teen Vogue*. These all feature fashion, makeup tips, dating advice, and other topics of interest to middle school girls.

Magazines for kids should be attractive, with interesting articles. If they contain advertisements, those should be age appropriate. Many of the magazines for teens may not seem "suitable" for a library if they contain pictures of models posed too sexily, or ads that are coarse, like those found in the *WWE* magazine. Another "problem" with kids' magazines is that many of them are bimonthly—so you might ask whether it's worth the hassle and subscription cost for just six issues a year. Others just publish during the nine months of the school year; public libraries often prefer magazines that are published monthly. Find out which magazines are available for children and 'tweens and might fit the interests of your community's young readers. For the very reluctant reader, or the 'tween who just doesn't want to read books at all, magazines can fill the bill.

Helpful Books and Web Sites on Graphic Novels

Graphic novels are still a new area in many libraries; luckily, some great reference books and several Web sites can help you find out more about this type of book, which is growing in popularity.

Brenner, Robin E. *Understanding Manga and Anime.* Westport, CT: Libraries Unlimited, 2007.

From the author of the Web site No Flying, No Tights, this guide to manga, the Japanese-style graphic novel, covers the history of this format and has an extensive list of titles to recommend to patrons.

Center for Cartoon Studies. www.cartoonstudies.org

The Center for Cartoon Studies publishes classic graphic novels and nonfiction graphic novels. Check out the recommendations.

Gorman, Michelle. *Getting Graphic! Using Graphic Novels to Promote Literacy with Teens and Preteens.* Westport, CT: Linworth, 2003.

This handy guide covers collection development of graphic novels and using and recommending this format to students. Entries include both grade levels and summaries of the recommended graphic novels listed.

Kannenberg, Gene. *500 Essential Graphic Novels: the Ultimate Guide.* New York: Collins Design, 2008.

If you don't know much about graphic novels, this book can be a big help in figuring out which graphic novels to buy for your library. He recommends a wide variety of popular graphic novels and provides some age designations to help you figure out if a graphic novel is for 'tweens or older teens and adults.

No Flying, No Tights. www.noflyingnotights.com/

A great Web site to find lists of graphic novels to suggest to teens; you can also choose the "Sidekicks" section for graphic novels for younger readers.

Papercutz. www.papercutz.com/

Papercutz is a popular publisher of graphic novels; check out the reading suggestions.

Pawuk, Michael. *Graphic Novels: A Genre Guide to Comic Books, Manga and More.* Westport, CT: Libraries Unlimited, 2007.

Nine main groupings of graphic novels are covered in this guide, part of the Genreflecting Advisory Series. From horror to humor, fantasy to nonfiction, each entry has an annotation and grade level designation to help library staff and patrons find the right graphic novel for any reader.

Scholastic Graphix. www.scholastic.com/graphix/

Graphix is the graphic novel subdivision of Scholastic books, and this site offers lots of recommendations.

GRAPHIC NOVELS FOR YOUNGER CHILDREN, AGES SIX TO TEN

Davis, Eleanor. *Stinky.*

Gownley, Jimmy. *Amelia Rules! What Makes You Happy.*

Guibert, Emmanuel. <u>Sardine in Outer Space</u> series.

Holm, Jennifer L. <u>Babymouse</u> series.

Morse, Scott. <u>Magic Pickle</u> series.

Runton, Andy. <u>Owly</u> series.

Sfar, Joann. <u>Little Vampire</u> series.

Smith, Jeff. <u>Bone</u> series.

Various. <u>W.I.T.C.H.</u> series.

GRAPHIC NOVELS FOR 'TWEENS, AGES NINE TO THIRTEEN

Abadzis, Nick. *Laika.*

Bendis, Brian M. *Ultimate Spiderman.*

Brennan, Michael. *Electric Girl.*

Colfer, Eoin. *Artemis Fowl: The Graphic Novel.*

Dixon, Franklyn. <u>The Hardy Boys</u> graphic novel series.

Gaiman, Neil. *Coraline: The Graphic Novel.*

Hale, Shannon, and Dean Hale. *Rapunzel's Revenge.*

Keene, Carolyn. <u>Nancy Drew</u> graphic novel series.

Kesel, Barbara. <u>Meridian</u> series.

Lat. *Kampung Boy.*

Lat. *Town Boy.*

Martin, Ann. M. <u>Babysitter Club</u> graphic novel series.

Medley, Linda. *Castle Waiting.*

Miyazaki, Hayao. <u>Nausicaa of the Valley of the Wind</u> series.

Ottaviani, Jim. *T-Minus: The Race to the Moon.*

Patterson, James, and Leopoldo Gout. *Daniel X: Alien Hunter.*

Siegel, Siena Cherson. *To Dance: A Ballerina's Graphic Novel.*

Smith, Jeff. <u>Bone</u> series.

Soo, Kean. <u>Jellaby</u> series.

Stine, R. L. <u>Goosebumps</u> graphic novel series.

Tezuka, Osamu. <u>Astro Boy</u> series.

Torres, J. <u>Alison Dare</u> series.

Various. <u>Totally Spies</u> series.

Varon, Sara. *Robot Dreams.*

Yang, Gene. *American Born Chinese.*

Chapter 12

Promoting Books to Children and 'Tweens

There will be times when a young person is wandering around the library, but not coming up to your desk to ask for help. Or you may have a class visiting the library on a field trip, and you would like to promote some books to the group. In those cases, you will need some techniques for promoting books to children and 'tweens. Librarians today are becoming more savvy when it comes to marketing products and services, and that includes readers' advisory–related promotions. A few common techniques are discussed in this chapter.

Booktalks

Booktalks are a great, quick, and easy way to hand-sell books to students. Think of them as the "sneak preview" of the book; they work the way trailers in movie theaters do to excite viewers to come back for other films. After you have read a book, write up a two- or three-paragraph description of the plot and characters, focusing on promoting the book to young readers. A booktalk is not a book review or a summary; it is really a very brief persuasive speech on what the book is about and why it is appealing.

Here is a sample booktalk on Gary Paulsen's *Hatchet*:

> A boy is the only survivor of a small plane crash. He is alone in the woods, with just a hatchet. He has to make fire, find food, get away from wild animals, and try to survive until he can be found or until he can make his way out of the forest. This action-packed story has element's of the TV shows *Survivor* and *Lost*, and is a real page-turner.

Following are some important tips to remember when delivering booktalks:

- Keep it brief (about 90 seconds).

- Booktalk more than novels—use nonfiction and graphic novels, too!

- Never give away the ending of a book.

- Use humor when appropriate.

- Relate a book to a TV show or movie—"This adventure story has elements of *Survivor* in it, crossed with *Lost!*"

- Get the students to tell you their favorite books in response to the booktalk.

- Encourage students to booktalk with each other.

- Booktalk at the reference desk and in the stacks, not just in formal presentations.

- Use "tech to talk": try booktalk podcasts, blogging, and so on to get your message across.

There are several books that describe how to write and perform booktalks, including *Booktalking That Works* by Jennifer Bromann and books by Joni Bodart. Bodart is considered the first and foremost proponent of the booktalk. Be sure to check out her Web site, www.thebooktalker.com/. She provides many examples of booktalks you can use as the format for your own.

Another great resource on how to write a booktalk is the Web site nancykeane.com/, compiled by Nancy Keane. She lists thousands of booktalks of children's books. She also has a great "how-to" section on her FAQ page, a podcast, and links to other great resources. Keane also has written a book with Terence W. Cavanaugh, *The Tech-Savvy Booktalker*, which is listed at the end of this chapter.

As noted in the list above, one key rule of thumb with a booktalk is to NEVER give away the ending of the book. Booktalks can be delivered casually, when helping a student find a fun book to read, or they can be given at the end of a school tour. You can also do a book auction: give thirty-second talks on several books, with students raising their hands to "buy" that book for checkout.

Follow up your booktalks with handouts or bookmarks that list the titles. Keep these at the reference desk in case a 'tween has forgotten the one you distributed when you first did the booktalks. Prepare other booklists on paper—these are still very effective readers' advisory tools. Include lists by genre ("Great 'Tween Mysteries"), of read-alikes (" 'Tween Vampire Novels—If you like *Twilight* Try These Books"), by grade, for 'tween guys, for 'tween girls, etc. Also try to do easy displays of a new genre or category to "market" these books; you don't have to do fancy bulletin boards to do a book display. Booklists and displays are discussed further below.

YouTube Booktalks

For more on booktalks, such as how they work in front of a class or group of students, look at some of the booktalks on YouTube (www.youtube.com/). In the search box, type in "booktalks for children" to bring up several examples of booktalks done in classrooms. You can also post some of your own booktalks there.

Podcasts

Booktalking in person is a tried-and-true method of "advertising" books to children, 'tweens, and teens. But some libraries have taken it to the next level—booktalks on the library Web site in the form of a podcast, so they can reach those at home. Basically, a podcast is a recorded version of the booktalk, which the Web site user can listen to. Many libraries have noticed that their Web sites are like an extra branch library, open twenty-four hours a day, available to many library users who may not be able to come to the library often. So podcasts and other material you put on the library Web site are a great way to reach out to new library users. Ask your library's Webmaster if it is possible to add podcast booktalks to the Web site.

Recording the Podcast

Before you record your podcast, write out the booktalk the way you would if you were going to do it in a classroom. Practice reading it aloud a few times, to get the rhythm of your speech and to see if you need to change anything. Be sure to write out any quotes you plan to use, so you don't have to grab the book while you are recording, which would cause an unnecessary pause in your speech.

Once you feel satisfied with your booktalk in written form, and you have practiced it a few times, get ready to record it. Avoid a lot of pauses (the listener will think you lost your place), and avoid "you know," "uh," or other speech hiccups that can annoy the listener. When you are ready to record, just use your regular tone of voice and volume, as if you were speaking to a friend over the telephone. Try not to rush—that is a common mistake when recording podcasts.

To hear some podcast booktalks, check out www.podfeed.net/podcast/Bookwink+booktalks+for+kids/10030. This Web site has some great children's booktalk podcasts, done by a teacher. She aims the booktalks at grades three to eight and includes nonfiction books, which can be a refreshing change!

Booklists and Bibliographies

When it comes to preparing booklists, there are to two things in my background I bring to the task: journalism and restaurant management. Journalism is really the type of writing we do for bibliographies. You want to give the "who, what, when, where, and how" in the fewest possible words. And you want to write "advertising copy"—you are "selling" the books by describing the stories with active verbs, creating the "I need that" impulse in your customers. Use active verbs, such as "He struggled, overcoming the challenge of being alone in the forest with only a hatchet to help him make shelter, find food, and defend himself from wild animals." That type of description can grab the most reluctant reader.

A booklist is much like a "menu" for goods books available at your library. Like any good menu, it should contain brief, pertinent information that will "sell" the item. As many a marketing executive has said, you want to sell the "sizzle," not the steak; that is, you don't need to tell the customer every "ingredient" in the book, and you MUST NOT GIVE AWAY THE ENDING! You just want to give customers the "flavor" of the book! You want your "menu" descriptions to be short and snappy, enticing the reader to think that item might be of interest. And of course you don't want to mislead the menu reader: don't describe a book that makes you cry, such as *Old Yeller*, by focusing on the funny parts, or make a book with sexual content like *Angus, Thongs, and Full Frontal Snogging* sound good to an eight-year-old.

Keeping Booklists Up-to-Date

Because bibliographies and lists are typed in a word processing program such as Word, it is easy to revise them when newer books on the subject or in a genre are published. For example, many novels in the same genre as <u>Harry Potter</u> have recently been published, in part to capitalize on its success, and you can simply update your <u>Harry Potter</u> read-alikes list every six months. The success of *Twilight* by Stephenie Meyer has inspired a flood of vampire-themed books for 'tweens and teens. If you made a *Twilight* read-alike handout when the book first came out, it is probably time to revise it.

Some handouts list the books in alphabetical order by title or author. You may prefer to list them randomly; that can work to encourage the patron to walk around the shelving area. If a list is in alphabetical order by author, only the first books may be chosen; if you mix the list up, patrons will browse more as they look for various authors.

Who Is the Audience?

At times you will make booklists for a variety of audiences, and some lists are designed to enhance a specific library program. For example, you may have a handout geared to parents, with helpful books on toilet training, getting a baby to sleep, and other issues, and distribute that handout at a toddler storytime to assist parents. Or you might create a handout on books for children by Asian American authors and illustrators and distribute it at your Lunar New Year program. Perhaps there is a popular homework assignment—make a handout on the new science experiment books if that is in demand.

Annotated or Not?

It is common for libraries to distribute annotated booklists, with a sentence or two describing the book, which can be an effective way to "sell" the book. Avoid beginning each annotation with "This book . . ."; that can get monotonous. Try to use an opening sentence that grabs the reader's attention. Annotations should be short, snappy, catchy, and active. A method used in Hollywood to describe movies and TV shows is to break down description into the "high concept"; that is, use clear buzz words that evoke an image. For example, <u>Goosebumps</u> are funny, scary stories with twist endings like *The Twilight Zone*. *Out of the Dust* is a poignant story of a girl and her father surviving the Dust Bowl and poverty of the Great Depression. I am sure you can think of other examples. Often I write the annotation in the form of a question; for example, for

Natalie Babbitt's *Tuck Everlasting* I use: "Will Winnie drink from the fountain of youth so she can stay young forever and be with Jesse Tuck, and will they evade the evil man in the yellow suit who is following them?" I find it helpful to remember that annotation writing isn't a literary endeavor, it is journalism. It is similar to writing advertising copy.

Booklists without annotations can also be useful; often the titles are enough to sell the books. Such lists are almost like shopping lists, and the theme is what sells the books. For example, a list of vampire-themed 'tween novels won't need descriptions for each book; the *Twilight* fan will look at the book jacket and decide if a book is interesting.

Displays

Because displays are a passive way of promoting books—librarians don't often talk to a child or 'tween at the display area to offer readers' advisory—you may forget that displays can be a great way to promote areas of the collection. These displays do not have to be labor intensive; in fact, simple and clear can be more effective than a cluttered bulletin board.

If you find your poetry books are gathering dust, move them to a display area with a colorful poster—many publishers' catalogs or professional library journals include free posters. Or make a simple but professional sign using a computer to spell out what is being displayed.

Displays for Teachable Moments

There will be teachable moments that inspire a display—maybe something in the news will lead you to make a display on climate change and global warming, or recycling, or on a country that is suddenly in the news. A free poster may inspire a display. Use old maps as the background for a bulletin board, with simple lettering, to promote books about the country shown in the map, including folktales, novels, poetry, and nonfiction relating to the country.

Displays are effective because the books face outward—book jackets can do a lot to sell the books. On the shelves, the book jackets are not visible until a patron pulls the books off the shelf. In addition to your book displays, try some "face out" book displays at the shelving area, if you have room.

Change the displays at least once a month, more frequently if possible. If items on a display aren't moving, try another type of book or another subject, and see what "sells." Experiment with unusual topics that have a lot of kid appeal, such as "gross" stuff, horror, comic collections, or hands-on topics like paper airplanes and origami. Besides the common genres of fiction, try more unusual topics such as novels turned into films, or novels set in your state, to grab the attention of reluctant readers.

Book Discussion Groups

Book discussion groups are a rewarding and fun program for libraries, whether for adults, teens, or 'tweens. Usually these groups are for those old enough to be independent readers; I find that children in the fourth and fifth grades can make up a great discussion group. These groups often meet once a month to discuss a book everyone has read; school libraries may adapt their plans for students to meet weekly or more often, to discuss a chapter or two at each meeting until the book is finished. Book discussion groups can be a great way to ask 'tweens what books they are reading and what they like, and you can use those responses with other children and 'tweens when doing readers' advisory.

How to Organize a Book Discussion Group

Shireen Dodson's *The Mother Daughter Book Club* is a helpful source on planning and organizing a book discussion group. Other resources that can help you start a book discussion group at your library can be found at the Multnomah County (Oregon) Library Web site (www. multcolib.org). It has a section under the Readers tab for kids' books, called "Talk It Up," which describes how to start a club and lists ideas for more than 150 novels for kids to read, along with discussion questions. Many publishers' Web sites also have outlines for using a book in a discussion group; my favorites are at the HarperCollins and Scholastic sites.

One criticism many children's librarians hear is that book discussion groups only appeal to girls; that has not been true at my library. We have as many boys as girls in our fourth- and fifth-grade club and in our middle school club (grades 6, 7, and 8). This could be because we always have refreshments (often chosen to go along with something in that month's book) and do a hands-on activity like a game or craft to go with the book. We also alternate each month between girl and boy protagonists. Boys will read books with girl main characters if the book interests them, like *Because of Winn Dixie* by Kate DiCamillo. Often you can find books with boys and girls as equal characters, such as Katherine Paterson's *Bridge to Terabithia* or E. L. Konigsburg's *A View from Saturday*.

Do Hands-on Activities

Activities should tie in with that month's book. You may be surprised by what students enjoy—we had the kids play marbles to go along with a book set in the early 1900s, and they loved the game! Cooking is always a winner, whether it is making chocolate no-bake cookies to go along with *Charlie and the Chocolate Factory* or making caramel apples to go along with the county fair theme we did for *Charlotte's Web.* There may be times guest speakers go along with a book; we had a botanist bring in silkworms for *Project Mulberry* by Linda Sue Park. When we discussed a novel set during the Great Depression, our eighty-year-old security guard brought in photos and toys from his childhood and talked about what it was like to grow up at that time.

Publicity and Budgeting

Publicity and budgeting are fundamental to the success of a book discussion group. It is natural to assume that kids who regularly read and visit the library are a key demographic for a discussion group, but be sure to promote the group to others, targeting flyers to teachers and school librarians who know and can identify avid readers; homeschoolers who may want the social interaction of an organized group; and organizations like Scouts, the Boys and Girls Club, etc.

Even if you get great attendance, it can be a challenge to keep the kids "on task"—talking about that month's book. Having prepared discussion questions can help students keep notes as they read the book, then have something to say when they bring the questions and answers to the meeting. It can also help you as the facilitator remember what to ask.

Another great resource for planning your club is *The Teen-Centered Book Club: Readers into Leaders* by Bonnie Kunzel and Constance Hardesty. Even though it is aimed at librarians working with teens, it is easy to adapt most of their ideas to 'tweens, especially the organization plans, publicity, and discussion techniques; even some of their book suggestions will work with 'tweens. It is common for teen book clubs to allow teens to nominate and vote on what books will be read at upcoming meetings; you could try that with book clubs for fourth and fifth graders, too.

Using Summer Reading Program Themes to Promote Books

Most public libraries have a summer reading program for children; even some school libraries conduct a summer reading game of some sort. These programs encourage and reward children and 'tweens for reading over summer vacation, but very few have a required reading list. The idea is that children should read what they want to read; the whole concept of a summer reading program is to promote recreational reading. There is statistical evidence that summer reading helps a child avoid "the summer slide," which means that children who don't read during the summer start the new school year at a lower reading level than they had at the end of the previous school year.

Currently forty-five states are members of the Collaborative Summer Library Program (CSLP) cooperative, which provides a new theme each year for children and teens. Using the CSLP materials is an efficient way to conduct a summer reading program, but even if your library is not a member, summer reading can be a great way to promote books and do readers' advisory. Whatever the theme is for your summer reading game, have lists and displays to promote related books. Also promote books in general—popular best sellers, books based on movies, and so forth. At the end of this chapter are lists of great 'tween books related to CSLP's 2010 and 2011 themes. If your state is a member, be sure to check out the Web site (www.cslpreads.org/) to see future themes, so you can purchase related books ahead of time.

Helpful Books and Web Sites on Promoting Books to Youth

There are several reference books and Web sites that can help you with techniques for book promotion. A few are listed here:

ALA/ALSC Notable Children's Booklists. www.ala.org/ ala/mgrps/divs/alsc/awardsgrants/childrensnotable/ notablechibooks/index.cfm

Books chosen by children's librarians as best each year are listed here; these lists also include the Newbery, Caldecott, Coretta Scott King, and Pura Belpre award and honor books.

Book Adventure. www.bookadventure.org/

As mentioned in chapter 1, this is hands-down the easiest site to use for a library staff member unfamiliar with doing readers' advisory for youth. It is operated by the tutoring company Sylvan Learning, but it is free, and you don't have to register to use it. Click on "Kids Zone," then on "Book Finder." You will find an easy-to-use menu of topics; enter the grade level you are interested in and whether you want fiction or nonfiction. Then click the genres or topics you want—mystery, adventure, etc. The site will list twenty-five books fitting those criteria. Your library may not carry all of the books on the list, but it should have many of them, because they are often award winners or books by popular children's authors. Show 'tweens how to use the site; they will "play" on the Web site and find lots of great titles to choose from.

The Booktalker—Joni Bodart. www.thebooktalker.com/

Maintained by the premiere proponent of the booktalk, this Web site features many booktalks written by Dr. Bodart, who is a popular professor of library science at San Jose State University.

Bromann, Jennifer. *Booktalking That Works.* New York: Neal-Schuman Publishers, 2001.

A longtime youth services librarian explains step by step how to write and use booktalks with teens; her advice can be easily adapted to booktalks for 'tweens and children.

Cavanaugh, Terence W., and Nancy J. Keane. *The Tech-Savvy Booktalker: A Guide for 21st Century Educators.* Westport, CT: Libraries Unlimited, 2008.

Aimed at middle and high school teachers and librarians, this booktalking manual also describes how to use technology, such as video or podcasts, when doing booktalks.

Dodson, Shireen. *The Mother Daughter Book Club.* New York: HarperCollins, 1997.

Dodson is an assistant director for the Smithsonian and a mother; she wrote this guide for parents. Many librarians also find it very useful in starting a book discussion group.

Kunzel, Bonnie, and Hardesty, Constance. *The Teen-Centered Book Club: Readers into Leaders.* Westport, CT: Libraries Unlimited, 2006.

Two young adult librarians offer a useful guide that demonstrates that book clubs for youth are more about the participants than about the books. They include great tips on setting up the club, selecting books, and detailing activities. Their advice is easily adapted for use with 'tweens.

Langemack, Chapple. *Booktalker's Bible: How to Talk about the Books You Love to Any Audience.* Westport, CT: Libraries Unlimited, 2003.

Fail-safe techniques on performing booktalks will help even those with stage fright learn to present booktalks to children, 'tweens, and teens. Funny anecdotes and plenty of sample booktalks are included in this handy guide.

LaPerriere, Jenny, and Trish Christensen. *Merchandising Made Simple: Using Standards and Dynamic Displays to Boost Circulation.* Westport, CT: Libraries Unlimited, 2008.

Learn to make dynamic displays with materials you already have on hand, or can acquire at little cost, to promote books to a wide variety of readers.

Multnomah County Library, Oregon. www.multcolib.org/ kids/booklists/

Another helpful Web site is offered by the Multnomah County Library in Oregon. It is packed with reading lists, which you can print out and use with students.

Nancy Keane's Booktalks. nancykeane.com/

Over 5,000 ready-to-use booktalks for grades K–12!

Publishers Weekly Bestseller Lists. www.publishersweekly. com/bestsellerslist/11.html?channel=bestsellers

Check out the weekly children's best seller list; about half the books are for teens.

Scholastic Books. www.scholastic.com/librarians/

Scholastic's Web site has a great area for librarians. It contains book discussion guides, booktalks (including some video clips of booktalks), lists of books by topic, and an easy to use search feature. You can search for a topic such as mystery, then narrow your search by grade. Searching "Mysteries" for grades 3 to 5 resulted in 2,000 suggestions!

SUMMER READING PROGRAM BOOKLISTS

2010 Water Theme: "Make a Splash—Read!"

Books for Younger Children

Aardema, Verna. *Bringing the Rain to Kapiti Plain.*

Ardizzone, Edward. <u>Tim</u> series.

Atkins, Jeannine. *Get Set! Swim!*

Base, Graeme. *The Water Hole.*

Brown, Marc. *D.W. All Wet.*

Calhoun, Mary. *Henry the Sailor Cat.*

Cash, Megan. *I Saw the Sea and the Sea Saw Me.*

Elya, Susan Middleton. *Bebe Goes to the Beach.*

Kvasnosky, Laura McGee. *Frank and Izzy Set Sail.*

Lasky, Kathryn. *Pirate Bob.*

Lee, Suzy. *Wave.*

London, Jonathan. *Froggy Learns to Swim.*

London, Jonathan. *Where the Big Fish Are.*

Lund, Deb. *Dinosailors.*

Mahy, Margaret. *The Great White Man-Eating Shark: A Cautionary Tale.*

Mammano, Julie. *Rhinos Who Surf.*

McCloskey, Robert. *Burt Dow, Deep-water Man.*

Metzger, Steve. *Five Little Sharks Swimming in the Sea.*

Mills, Claudia. *Gus and Grandpa Go Fishing.*

O'Neill, Alexis. *Loud Emily.*

Oppel, Kenneth. *Peg and the Whale.*

Palmer, Helen. *A Fish out of Water.*

Pallotta, Jerry. *Dory Story.*

Parr, Todd. *Otto Goes to the Beach.*

Pfister, Marcus. *Rainbow Fish* series.

Rockwell, Ann. *Ferryboat Ride.*

Rodriguez, Edel. *Sergio Makes a Splash.*

Sierra, Judy. *Ballyhoo Bay.*

Sobel, June. *Shiver Me Letters: A Pirate ABC.*

Stock, Catherine. *An Island Summer.*

Sturges, Philemon. *This Little Pirate.*

Watt, Melanie. *Scaredy Squirrel at the Beach.*

Wells, Rosemary. *Edward in Deep Water.*

Winton, Tim. *The Deep.*

'Tween Fiction

Ardagh, Philip. *Terrible Times.*

Avi. *The True Confessions of Charlotte Doyle.*

Babbitt, Natalie. *Tuck Everlasting.*

Carbone, Elisa. *Blood on the River.*

Carbone, Elisa. *Storm Warriors.*

Cooper, Susan. *Victory.*

Creech, Sharon. *The Wanderer.*

DeFelice, Cynthia C. *Death at Devil's Bridge.*

Dunmore, Helen. Ingo series.

Farmer, Nancy. *A Girl Named Disaster.*

Fleischman, Sid. *The Ghost in the Noonday Sun.*

Fleischman, Sid. *The Giant Rat of Sumatra or Pirates Galore.*

Harlow, Joan Hiatt. *Thunder from the Sea.*

Hausman, Gerald. *Tom Cringle: The Pirate and the Patriot.*

Haydon, Elizabeth. *The Floating Island: The Lost Journals of Ven Polypheme.*

Hesse, Karen. *The Music of Dolphins.*

Hesse, Karen. *Stowaway.*

Hoffman, Alice. *Aquamarine.*

Johansen, V. K. *Torrie and the Pirate Queen.*

Kessler, Liz. Emily Windsnap series.

Klise, Kate. *Regarding the Bathrooms: A Privy to the Past.*

Klise, Kate. *Regarding the Fountain.*

Klise, Kate. *Regarding the Sink.*

L'Engle, Madeleine. *A Ring of Endless Light.*

Mahy, Margaret. *The Pirates' Mixed-Up Voyage: Dark Doings in the Thousand Islands.*

Meyer, L. A. Bloody Jack series.

O'Dell, Scott. *The Dark Canoe.*

O'Dell, Scott. *Island of the Blue Dolphin.*

Paulsen, Gary. *Voyage of the Frog.*

Peck, Dale. *Drift House: The First Voyage.*

Philbrick, Rodman. *The Young Man and the Sea.*

Salisbury, Graham. *Lord of the Deep.*

Sperry, Armstrong. *Call It Courage.*

Steig, William. *Abel's Island.*

Taylor, Theodore. *The Cay.*

Thiele, Colin. *Shadow Shark.*

White, Ellen Emerson. *Voyage of the Great Titanic: The Diary of Margaret Ann Brady, R.M.S. Titanic, 1912.*

Whybrow, Ian. *Little Wolf, Terror of the Shivery Sea.*

Williams, Barbara. *Titanic Crossing.*

2011 World Travel Theme: "Discover the World @ Your Library"

Books for Younger Children

Averill, Esther. *Jenny Goes to Sea.*

Ayres, Katherine. *A Long Way.*

Base, Graeme. *The Water Hole.*

Bemelmans, Ludwig. Madeline collection.

Blackstone, Stella. *My Granny Went to Market.*

Brisson, Pat. *Kate on the Coast.*

Brisson, Pat. *Your Best Friend, Kate.*

Cooney, Barbara. *Miss Rumphius.*

Danziger, Paula. *You Can't Eat Your Chicken Pox, Amber Brown.*

Gilliland, Judith Heide. *Not in the House, Newton!*

Henkes, Kevin. *A Weekend for Wendell.*

Hyatt, Patricia. *Coast to Coast with Alice.*

Johnson, Crockett. *Harold and the Purple Crayon.*

Johnson, D. B. *Henry Hikes to Hitchburg.*

Joyce, Susan. *Post Card Passages.*

LeMarche, Jim. *The Raft.*

Lester, Helen. *Tacky in Trouble.*

Lobel, Anita. *Away from Home.*

MacLachlan, Patricia. *All the Places to Love.*

McCloskey, Robert. *Time of Wonder.*

Morris, Ann. *Bread, Bread, Bread.*

Morris, Ann. *Hats, Hats, Hats.*

Morris, Ann. *Shoes, Shoes, Shoes.*

Pattison, Darcy. *The Journey of Oliver K. Woodman.*

Potter, Giselle. *The Year I Didn't Go to School.*

Priceman, Marjorie. *How to Make a Cherry Pie and See the U.S.A.*

Priceman, Marjorie. *How to Make an Apple Pie and See the World.*

Rohmann, Eric. *My Friend Rabbit.*

Rylant, Cynthia. *Tulip Sees America.*

Scillian, Devin. *P Is for Passport: A World Alphabet.*

Teague, Mark. *The Secret Shortcut.*

Tunnell, Michael O. *Mailing May.*

Uegaki, Chieri. *Suki's Kimono.*

Walters, Virginia. *Are We There Yet, Daddy?*

Williams, Vera B. *Stringbean's Trip to the Shining Sea.*

'Tween Fiction

Burnford, Sheila. *The Incredible Journey.*

Creech, Sharon. *The Wanderer.*

Curtis, Christopher Paul. *The Watsons Go to Birmingham—1963.*

Cushman, Karen. *Rodzina.*

Danziger, Paula. *United Tates of America.*

DiCamillo, Kate. *The Miraculous Journey of Edward Tulane.*

DuBois, William Pene. *The Twenty-One Balloons.*

Feiffer, Jules. *A Barrel of Laughs, a Vale of Tears.*

Fleischman, Sid. *By the Great Horn Spoon!*

Glaser, Linda. *Bridge to America.*

Goscinny, Rene. *Nicholas on Vacation.*

Haddix, Margaret Peterson. *Takeoffs and Landings.*

Hobbs, Will. *Crossing the Wire.*

Hobbs, Will. *Down the Yukon.*

Peck, Richard. *Fair Weather.*

Roberts, Willo Davis. *What Could Go Wrong?*

Robertson, Keith. *Henry Reed's Journey.*

Ryan, Pamela MuZoz. *Esperanza Rising.*

Smith, Roland. *The Captain's Dog: My Journey with the Lewis and Clark Tribe.*

Spooner, Michael. *Daniel's Walk.*

Stewart, Trenton. *The Mysterious Benedict Society and the Perilous Journey.*

Vining, Elizabeth Gray. *Adam of the Road.*

Whelan, Gloria. *Parade of Shadows.*

Winkler, Henry. *Barfing in the Backseat: How I Survived My Family Road Trip.*

Suggested Readings

Ada, Alma Flor. *A Magical Encounter: Latino Children's Literature in the Classroom.* 2nd ed. Boston: Allyn and Bacon, 2003.

Anderson, Sheila B., ed. *Serving Young 'Tweens and Teens.* Westport, CT: Libraries Unlimited, 2007.

Atwell, Nancie. *The Reading Zone: How to Help Kids Become Skilled, Passionate, Habitual, Critical Readers.* New York: Scholastic Teaching Resources, 2007.

Barr, Catherine, and John T. Gillespie. *Best Books for Children: Preschool through Grade 6.* 9th ed. Westport, CT: Libraries Unlimited, 2010.

Barstow, Barbara, Lelsie Molnar, and Judith Riggle. *Beyond Picture Books.* 3rd ed. Westport, CT: Libraries Unlimited, 2007.

Baxter, Kathleen A., and Marcia Agness Kochel. *Gotcha Good!: Nonfiction Books to Get Kids Excited About Reading.* Westport, CT: Libraries Unlimited, 2008.

Bettelheim, Bruno. *The Uses of Enchantment: The Meaning and Importance of Fairy Tales.* New York: Penguin, 1991.

Bettelheim, Bruno, and Karen Zelan. *On Learning to Read: The Child's Fascination with Meaning..* New York: Penguin, 1991.

Brenner, Robin E. *Understanding Manga and Anime.* Westport, CT: Libraries Unlimited, 2007.

Bromann, Jennifer. *Booktalking That Works.* New York: Neal-Schuman Publishers, 2001.

Cavanaugh, Terence W., and Nancy J. Keane. *The Tech-Savvy Booktalker: A Guide for 21st Century Educators.* Westport, CT: Libraries Unlimited, 2008.

Cole, Pam B. *Young Adult Literature in the 21st Century.* New York: McGraw-Hill, 2009.

Day, Frances Ann. *Latina and Latino Voices in Literature: Lives and Works Updated and Expanded.* Santa Barbara, CA: Greenwood Press, 2003.

Dodson, Shireen. *The Mother Daughter Book Club.* New York: HarperCollins, 1997.

Dresang, Eliza. *Radical Change: Books for Youth in a Digital Age.* New York: H.W. Wilson, 1999.

Freeman, Judy. *Books Kids Will Sit Still for 3: A Read-Aloud Guide.* Westport, CT: Libraries Unlimited, 2006.

Gillespie, John T. *The Children's and Young Adult Literature Handbook: A Research and Reference Guide.* Westport, CT: Libraries Unlimited, 2005.

Glazer, Joan I., and Cyndi Giorgis. *Literature for Young Children.* 5th ed. Upper Saddle River, NJ: Prentice Hall, 2004.

Gorman, Michelle. *Getting Graphic! Using Graphic Novels to Promote Literacy with Teens and Preteens.* Westport, CT: Linworth, 2003.

Hearne, Betsy. *Choosing Books for Children.* 3rd ed. Chicago: University of Chicago Press, 1999.

Hopkins, Lee Bennett. *Pass the Poetry, Please!* 3rd ed. New York: HarperCollins, 1998.

Horning, Kathleen T. *From Cover to Cover: Evaluating and Reviewing Children's Books.* New York: HarperCollins, 1997.

Kannenberg, Gene. *500 Essential Graphic Novels: The Ultimate Guide.* New York: Collins Design, 2008.

Kunzel, Bonnie, and Constance Hardesty. *The Teen-Centered Book Club: Readers into Leaders.* Westport, CT: Libraries Unlimited, 2006.

Langemack, Chapple. *Booktalker's Bible: How to Talk about the Books You Love to Any Audience.* Westport, CT: Libraries Unlimited, 2003.

LaPerriere, Jenny, and Trish Christensen. *Merchandising Made Simple: Using Standards and Dynamic Displays to Boost Circulation.* Westport, CT: Libraries Unlimited, 2008.

Lesesne, Teri S. *Naked Reading: Uncovering What Tweens Need to Become Lifelong Readers.* Portland, ME: Stenhouse, 2006.

Lewis, Valerie V., and Walter M. Mayes. *Valerie and Walter's Best Books for Children: A Lively, Opinionated Guide—Revised and Updated.* New York: HarperCollins, 2004.

Lima, Carolyn W., and John A. Lima. *A to Zoo: Subject Access to Children's Picture Books.* 7th ed. Westport, CT: Libraries Unlimited, 2005.

Lynch-Brown, Carol, and Carl M. Tomlinson. *Essentials of Children's Literature.* 6th ed. Boston: Allyn and Bacon, 2008.

Odean, Kathleen. *Great Books for Boys*. New York: Ballantine Books, 1998.

Odean, Kathleen. *Great Books for Girls*. New York: Ballantine Books, 2002.

Pawuk, Michael. *Graphic Novels: A Genre Guide to Comic Books, Manga and More*. Westport, CT: Libraries Unlimited, 2007.

Price, Anne, and Juliette Yaakov. *Children's Catalog*. 18th ed. New York: H.W. Wilson, 2001.

Rand, Donna, and Toni Trent Parker. *Black Books Galore! Guide to More Great African American Children's Books*. New York: John Wiley & Sons, 2001.

Rand, Donna, Toni Trent Parker, and Sheila Foster. *Black Books Galore! Guide to Great African American Children's Books*. New York: John Wiley & Sons, 1998.

Smith, Henrietta M. *The Coretta Scott King Awards, 1970-2009: 40th Anniversary*. Chicago: American Library Association, 2009.

Straub, Susan, and K. J. Dell'Antonia, *Reading with Babies, Toddlers, and Twos: a Guide to Choosing, Reading, and Loving Books Together*. Naperville, IL: Sourcebooks, 2006.

Sutherland, Zena. *Children and Books*. 9th ed. New York: Longman, 1997.

Thomas, Rebecca L., and Catherine Barr. *Popular Series Fiction for K–6 Readers: A Reading and Selection Guide*. Westport, CT: Libraries Unlimited, 2005.

Tunnell, Michael O., and James S. Jacobs. *Children's Literature, Briefly*. 4th ed. Upper Saddle River, NJ: Pearson, 2008.

Various. *Intellectual Freedom for Children: The Censor is Coming*. Chicago: American Library Association, 2000.

Walter, Virginia A. *Children & Libraries: Getting it Right*. Chicago: American Library Association, 2001.

Woolls, Blanche. *The School Library Media Manager*. 3rd ed. Westport, CT: Libraries Unlimited, 2004.

Zbaracki, Matthew D. *Best Books for Boys: A Resource for Educators*. Westport, CT: Libraries Unlimited, 2008.

Index

About the Author

PENNY PECK has been a youth services librarian for over twenty-five years, doing readers' advisory and storytimes, and conducting innovative programs. Since 2002 she has also taught for San Jose State University's School of Library and Information Science. She is the author of *Crash Course in Children's Services* (Libraries Unlimited, 2006) and *Crash Course in Storytime Fundamentals* (Libraries Unlimited, 2008).